the Wood Stove & Fireplace Book

$1.25

the Wood Stove & Fireplace Book

Steve Sherman

Illustrated by Julia Older

BRYN MAWR PRESS

A special edition produced by
arrangement with Stackpole Books

THE WOOD STOVE AND FIREPLACE BOOK

Copyright © 1976 by
Steve Sherman

Published by
STACKPOLE BOOKS
Cameron and Kelker Streets
P.O. Box 1831
Harrisburg, Pa. 17105

*"Published simultaneously in Don Mills, Ontario, Canada
by Thomas Nelson & Sons, Ltd."*

Printed in the U.S.A.

Library of Congress Cataloging in Publication Data

Sherman, Steve, 1938-
    The wood stove and fireplace book.

    Includes index.
    1. Stoves, Wood.   2. Fireplaces.   I. Title.
TH7438.S53   644'.1   76-16790
ISBN 0-8117-2125-6

CONTENTS

the Wood Stove & Fireplace Book

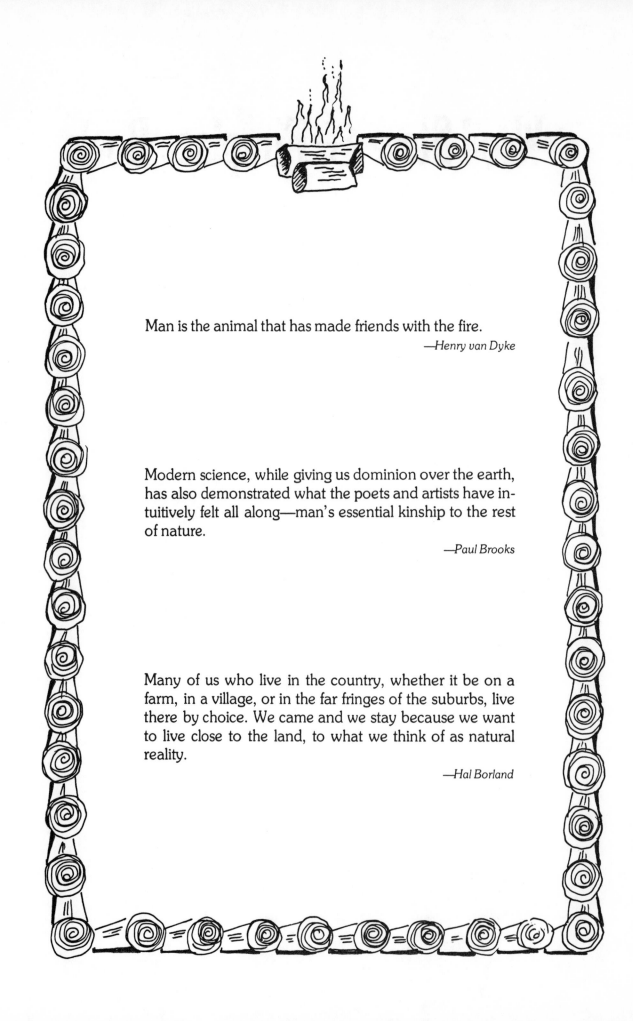

Man is the animal that has made friends with the fire.

—*Henry van Dyke*

Modern science, while giving us dominion over the earth, has also demonstrated what the poets and artists have intuitively felt all along—man's essential kinship to the rest of nature.

—*Paul Brooks*

Many of us who live in the country, whether it be on a farm, in a village, or in the far fringes of the suburbs, live there by choice. We came and we stay because we want to live close to the land, to what we think of as natural reality.

—*Hal Borland*

Chapter 1

FIRE

Fire is our essential friend. Without fire we could not fuse ores to make our farming tools, build power looms to weave the shirts on our backs, or shape hammer and nail to roof our heads. Food, clothing, and shelter. The absolute necessities. No matter how sophisticated we've made them or how far we've removed them from the source that starts them, we cannot have our food, clothing, and shelter without fire.

Yet by insulating ourselves as completely as we have from the basic origins of what sustains our very lives, we've often forgotten how important fire is. We've forgotten that being more aware of the basics of living attunes us better to the art of living. Besides, knowing something about fire not only makes its role in our lives clearer but also helps us to use it more effectively in wood-burning stoves and fireplaces.

And so for this vital, fundamental element that is the essence of this book, let's first of all take a quick look at it.

WHAT IT IS

Fire is the rapid oxidation of a combustible material. In other words, when a material reaches the temperature at which its molecules are agitated enough to break down so that oxygen is released to the air, that's fire.

Technically, you can't really see fire. What you see normally is the visible effect of fire—the flame. The perfect fire, then, in straight, hard-core, uninspiring, uncomforting scientific terms, is invisible.

A log burns because its outer surface is continually liquefied and vaporized. The more a log burns, the faster it shrinks, because the total surface area exposed to the oxidation process decreases.

Oxygen, fuel, and heat are the three ingredients in the fire recipe. Without one of them, no fire. Once a fire begins, it continues with the chimney effect. That is, as the fire heats the air surrounding the

birch-wood fires.) A flame without color would be the sign of a fire that burns nearly all its fuel.

WHERE FIRE COMES FROM

No matter where a people live, no matter how isolated they are from other tribes or nations, all groups of men and women have fire. The most primitive Stone Age people that anthropologists have discovered had fire. It can be said, then, that fire is a universal element of humankind. Not only that, but fire can be identified exclusively with man. No animals ever use fire.

How fire came to the hands of Homo sapiens is a matter of conjecture and interpretation, almost as diverse as the peoples on the earth, but variations of the ancient Greek myth are widespread. In that myth Prometheus, one of twelve Titan giants, stole fire from heaven and gave humankind its freedom

fire, the air expands and rises. New colder air with a fresh supply of oxygen rushes in to take the place of the heated, dissipating air. The cycle keeps revolving until the heat or the fuel decreases to zero. Keeping aware of this basic cycle is important later on in building and maintaining fires in both stoves and fireplaces, or, for that matter, in any situation.

Since the perfect fire has no flame, the flame therefore must be the result of imperfect burning. For all practical purposes, an imperfect burning is the normal light-giving fire we're used to seeing. What is interesting, however, is that the flame we usually associate as being the fire is actually microscopic particles of wood or other fuels that have not burned completely but are lightweight and incandescent enough to rise from the fire. (The color of a flame depends upon the temperature of the fire and burning material; blue-white propane flames, for example, are hotter than the orange-yellow

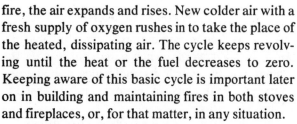

from the tyranny of the gods by giving us the power of flame. No longer was it the guarded treasure of the gods. It was fire that enabled us to rise above the other creatures of the planet and to become masters of the world, creative and godlike.

With such a prize handed to us, in our early history we worshiped fire for the freedom it gave us, as ancestors did in Iran, in the Feast of Fire in India, and in many other areas of the planet. The Toltecs of southern Mexico named their god of fire Xiuhtecuhtli and used what they called the Sun Stone for their calendar. The Druids of the British Isles called themselves Masters of Fire. Even we Americans revere the specialness of fire by symbolizing freedom through the flaming torch of the Statue of Liberty.

Heraclitus, the early Greek philosopher, considered fire the primal element of the universe, the material through and from which all else evolves. Empedocles, a follower of his, refined that idea to considering fire one of the four fundamental elements—fire, earth, air, water.

HOW TO MAKE FIRE

Theories state that primitive man probably first captured fire from lava or from trees set on fire by lightning or wildfires on the plains. Men took parts of these fires and nurtured them in their caves, used them to heat themselves and to cook their food.

Later they learned that friction causes heat and heat could become hot enough to ignite dry grass, shavings, or twigs. Fire drills and fire bows were in-

With pressure on top of the pole, the friction of the two pieces of wood against each other raised the temperature at their juncture until thin dry tinder grass smoldered and burst into flame. And freedom!

This treasure of living flame was the beginning of the headstrong drive of mankind to be like the gods, to reach for the temperature of the sun, and, eventually, to try to copy it with nuclear explosions.

vented that concentrated this friction into fires that could be controlled and predicted. Thin straps of animal hide on a curved stick were twisted around a small pole. With lots of elbow grease, the straps and bow turned the pole rapidly into a cup of soft wood.

MATCHES

Being able to carry fire in your pocket is the end product of innumerable experiments. Matches are now such common everyday items that we seldom if ever think of their implication of freedom, let alone convenience.

Matches weren't a gift from the gods but a long development of trial and error and success. The magical idea of carrying the secret of the gods wherever you went attracted early alchemists to the quest of solving this mystery. Hennig Brandt, a Hamburg alchemist, is credited with discovering the phosphorus match in 1669. His pocket fire resulted from coarse sheets of paper that were laminated with phosphorus. Then when small pieces of wood tipped with sulphur were yanked through the folded paper, fire appeared. It was magic at the time. It was also very expensive. Phosphorus cost $250 an ounce. So most seekers of fire continued with flint and steel matches, hard rock that sparked onto delicate kindling when struck onto pieces of metal.

Over the decades a variety of fire sticks were developed and most of them discarded. One was the Ethereal Match invented in France in 1781. Phosphorus-coated paper sealed in glass burst into flame when the glass was broken and exposed to oxygen.

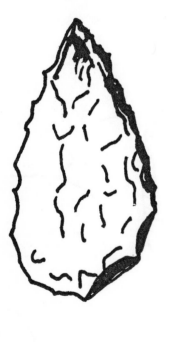

Other later designs were called the Pocket Luminary, the Instantaneous Light Box, Oxymuriated Matches, and, with the flair of early-day Madison Avenue advertising, the Electropneumatic Fire Producer.

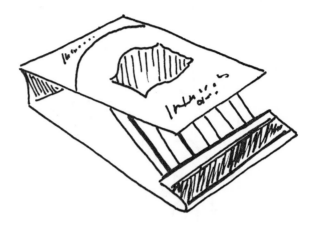

Not until 1827 did the basic friction match as we know it today appear in England. Pieces of wood—splinters, they were called—were dipped in antimony sulphide, potassium chlorate, a gum base, and starch. The splints were yanked through a coarse paper and, presto, fire! Or, popularly known then—Lucifers.

Three years later in France phosphorus was substituted for the antimony sulphide and, after certain refinements, such as the safety match that could not be ignited without striking it on a special box that had the other half of the fire ingredients, the modern match evolved.

One curiosity around the turn of the century was a match that would burn only to the midpoint of the splint. This way the flame wouldn't burn down to your fingers as you held it absentmindedly while you were talking. It was called the Drunkard's Match.

By 1911 the Diamond Match Company had developed sequisulphide of phosphorus, less dangerous in the manufacture of matches. The company shared its information with other match companies and thereby improved the safety of the entire industry.

Today the strike-anywhere kitchen matches, probably the most convenient of all forms, are part

of the 500 billion matches manufactured every year in the country. More than 300 billion book matches, first invented in 1892, are produced yearly and nearly all of them are given away free. The industry is so highly automated and the product at the top of its potential that the price of matches has remained virtually the same for generations.

The first machine to manufacture match splints was patented in 1841. Today machines can convert a block of pine into more than a million match splints an hour. Some matches are waterproofed and can be struck successfully even if submerged for eight hours—a military development for use during World War II in the tropics of the South Pacific.

The modern production of matches has remained the same even though electric lights have largely eliminated the necessity of candles, pilot lights in gas stoves and furnaces have done away with the once-ubiquitous boxes of red-tipped matches in the kitchen and basement, and cigarette lighters have replaced the direct pleasure of making fire between your fingers.

Maybe it's time to bring back some of that magical pleasure. With wood-burning stoves and fireplaces we can begin.

RESPECTING THE FLAME OF LIFE—AND DEATH

Honoring fire is more than merely discovering that it burns the curious the first time and fools the second time. Like the oppositional thumb, fire gives us a unique leap ahead in the evolutionary chain. It is our entrance to the future and at the same time it provides us with an assurance of the present.

Learning how we used fire in the past can give us not merely another dimension of pleasure but an entirely different perspective on the whole of life. Using fire in stoves and fireplaces to heat ourselves and our homes is not the panacea for a twentieth-century utopia. Yet it does give us an opportunity to be conscious of where our ultimate priorities should

be, to be aware of the mixture of the material simplicity and social complexity of fire and how it affects us, whether we know it or not. How much better to know it!

Like any friend, fire can turn against us if care isn't taken. It can burn and it can destroy, but with the slightest bit of information and attention fire can provide far more to the whole mosaic of our lives than we might anticipate from such a basic element of nature.

No matter in what proportion, using fire directly to heat our shelters helps to bring back to us our participation in the fundamentals of living. We don't have to return to a hunter economy to enjoy and learn from fire. In fact, no reason at all exists why computer analysts in the daytime cannot heat their homes in the evening by burning logs. What is important is that, no matter how complicated our lives, we still can learn from the simplicity of our essential friend.

The feather of the earth is my feather;
all that belongs to the earth belongs to me;
all that surrounds the earth surrounds me.

—*Navaho*

The forest depends on an unseen world of viruses,
molds, and bacteria, and the smaller forms of life
they nurture. All begins and ends here beneath
the trees, and those who are not aware, who have
only the grand point of view, miss the intimate
matrix of the design itself.

—*Sigurd Olson*

Trees are earth's endless effort to speak to the
listening heaven.

—*Rabindranath Tagore*

I think that I shall never see
a billboard lovely as a tree.
Perhaps, unless the billboards fall,
I'll never see a tree at all.

—*Ogden Nash*

Chapter 2

TREES

Besides fire, trees offer us probably the most useful resource tool of nature that man has bent and borrowed for his needs. Trees provide us with innumerable products that give us freedom, comfort, protection, and beauty in our everyday lives.

Because of this and the fact that we normally know too little about how this ordinary offspring of the earth grows and affects us, we should be aware of some of the wonders that trees unfold for us. Knowing some of the basics about the inner workings of trees—their densities, their fundamental differences, their best individual uses—can help to make wood heat part of the marrow of our lives.

THE MULTITUDES

Trees grow nearly everywhere on the face of the globe and assume such a wide spectrum of form that it is difficult for dendrologists, the tree specialists, to keep track of them. Trees range from quasi-shrubs to towering behemoths. They grow in every climate except extreme cold and extreme dryness. Even an all-encompassing definition of trees is hard to come by. The closest formal one is "a large, woody, long-lived plant with a well-developed trunk." The footnotes usually add that, even though some shrubs and trees overlap in definition, trees usually are considered to be a minimum of 12 feet in height. Some shrubs have one trunk and some trees more than one trunk, but the overall everyday vision of a tree includes one solid trunk of at least 3 inches in diameter, with branches that produce seeds for regeneration.

More than 50,000 species of trees exist in the world. Within the continental United States, the American Forestry Association totals 865 different species of trees native to our land; that is, they continue to reproduce in the wild.

Differences among these species are startling. Some of the giants within a particular species, such

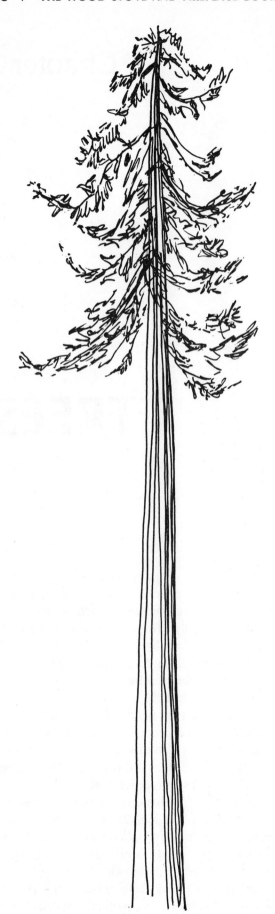

as the rusty blackhaw, never grow higher than 25 feet. Others, such as the Pacific Coast redwoods, grow beyond the 300-foot mark. One has reached nearly 370 feet in height.

Some trees reach maturity relatively early, such as the aspens before their one hundredth birthday, while the bristlecone pines in the White Mountains of California still live after 4,800 years, adding an inch to their girths every 100 years.

The bristlecone pines are few and highly prized and protected, but much of our country is studded with oaks and maples and hickories and black locusts—old standby trees that are the close friends of fire builders.

TREES EQUAL CIVILIZATION

Too few of us think of this as the Age of Trees and yet it is this in the fullest sense, far more than the so-called Age of the Atom or Age of Electricity. In all their multiple forms, trees are a direct part of our everyday lives. In fact, it can be said without any stretch of the imagination that trees form the basis of our civilization.

This sounds outlandish on the surface, but even a fast glance around our immediate environment shows this to be true. First of all, trees in their primary state give us beauty and shade (not to mention logs for fuel). In various other transformed

states, trees account for the building material of 75 percent of the total number of American houses, some of which have lasted for 200 and 300 years. Trees end up as chairs and dining room tables, floors, ceilings, garage doors, workbenches, steps, musical instruments, picture frames, pencils, clothespins, baskets, handles on kitchen utensils, stereo record player cabinets, broomsticks, and bookshelves.

In other forms, trees are processed into the paper upon which this book is printed, newspapers and magazines, dictionaries and pocketbooks, drinking cups, match sticks, charcoal for backyard barbecues, carton boxes, wrapping paper, bath-room tissue, and the nearly infinite line of products derived all the way back to the birches and pines and walnuts.

Literally no other workable material has been found for railroad ties (more than 20 million ties are replaced each year) and in that sense trees make it possible for rail freight and passenger traffic to move from state to state and across the continent. Telephone poles are made from trees, as are fence posts, bridges, piers, swings, wheelbarrows, hoes, rakes, and even women's shoes, cork or otherwise.

Pecans, walnuts, almonds, hickories, and most of the other nuts we eat come from trees. Many sea-sonings such as pepper and cinnamon come from

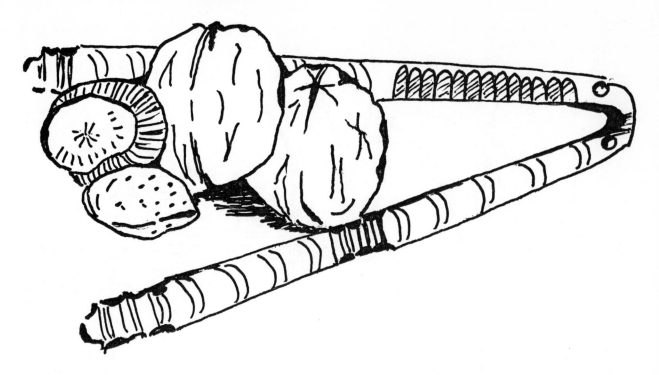

trees, as do the corks stuffed into wine bottles, rubber shaped for motor and bicycle wheels, and apples, oranges, grapefruit, lemons, pears, peaches, and pomegranates picked for the fruits we eat.

When tree wood is treated chemically and processed, it ends up in our hands as combs, photographic film, water pipes, and electrical tubes. From trees come cellulose that is the basis of acetates and explosives, that finds its way into kitchen sponges, building windows, cooking glass, and waterproof wrapping paper. Processed another way, cellulose from trees becomes rayon that can be finely spun to imitate cotton and wool and be sewn as shirts and slacks, seat covers and drapes.

Trees can be harvested for maple syrup and turpentine, products that reach us on the breakfast table, in paint thinner, or in bottles of medicine.

In short, endless is the list of ways in which trees become so essential that our society as we know it could in every sense of the word not exist without them. Actually, every American consumes about 450 pounds of tree products every year. Fortunately, trees are an invaluable renewable resource composed of little more than water, air, and soil nutrients, a gift outright from the earth. They've been around millennia before we ar-

rived—and they're doing fine. They're a real bargain. And to top it all off, nature has automated the entire growing process. You can't beat a deal like that.

HOW THEY GROW

The growth of trees and other plant life is the rock-bottom groundwork that allows all animal and human life to exist. Being the largest and most widespread of the plants, trees form the bulk of oxygen-producing organisms in the world.

Basically, trees and other chlorophyll-based plants live and grow by photosynthesis. Chlorophyll is the green blood in the leaves and needles of trees. To keep chlorophyll active, sunlight energy is needed to photosynthesize carbon dioxide and water into carbohydrates, the energy food. As a by-product of this conversion, oxygen is released from leaves and needles and dissipated into the atmosphere.

Photosynthesis in trees occurs only in the green leaves and needles, not the branches or trunks. Because of this, water and soil nutrients must rise from the root hairs to the larger root system, up through the trunk to the branches and limbs, and finally enter the leaves where the chlorophyll is contained.

It's a closed system. Without one ingredient—either the chlorophyll, sunlight, water, carbon dioxide, or nutrients—no conversion of the living process occurs. As a result, no oxygen would exist—and no us.

This simple process is basic to all plant life and yet it is not now fully understood by us. If artificial photosynthesis could be developed on a mass scale rather than merely in small laboratory experiments, as has been done, starvation on the planet earth would be eliminated. So far, however, the trees are keeping their secret.

BEHIND THE BARK

Like our own skin that is used partly to protect our vital organs, bark protects the inner life functions of a tree. Bark acts as an insulation against severe cold and heat, keeps moisture inside (in fact, bark is virtually moistureproof), shields the tree from diseases as well as burrowing chipmunks and squirrels, and is designed to grow and thicken as the tree itself expands in growth.

Like nearly all other parts of a tree, bark is useful to us. The most familiar bark product is cork from the cork oak native to the Mediterranean Sea region. This bark is cut for wine bottles and insulated jugs, rafts, furniture parts and wall facings. Latex, the source of rubber, comes from a different tree bark. Tannic acid in other barks is used in leather processing, inks, and dyes.

From the bark on in, the major sections of a tree consist of:

Bast

This extremely thin channel of cells transmits the sugar-rich sap from the leaves and needles to nourish the cambium and the root system.

Cambium

This equally thin, microscopic channel of living cells is the true life-sustaining heart of every tree. It circles every tree trunk, every branch and limb. It is highly productive in cell division and is the source of all the wood a tree generates from seedling to maturity. Cambium is the wellspring of life to a tree. It must constantly be fed the energy sap that leaves produce by photosynthesis. It follows, then, that when the leaves fall in autumn and winter, no tree growth occurs until spring and summer when the leaves return. Since cambium also nourishes and develops the bark, it feeds the tree in both directions, inward toward the woody section, outward toward the bark.

Sapwood

This larger visible section of the inner tree carries the sap water from the root hairs up through the woody channels to the leaves for photosynthesis. Sap is the basic fuel for the continued life of any tree. It consists of salts, acids, and sugars necessary

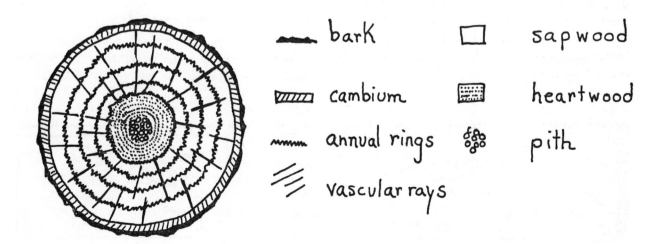

for reproduction of cells and seeds and is stored in ample supply in this outer, usually lighter-colored wood.

Heartwood

As a tree enlarges, all the old sapwood isn't necessary as a food conduit. This older section becomes the heartwood, which is usually, but not always, easily seen as darker in color. This section is often, as in oaks, resistant to rotting because it contains tannic acid. In softwood trees, such as the pines, the heartwood contains resin and is likewise usually more resistant to decay than the sapwood. Heartwood also forms the rigidity and strength of a tree, gives it stability and support.

Knots

Knots found in a tree trunk are merely early-growing branches that were enclosed by the expanding tree. Every tree, because it enlarges, has knots. They cannot be avoided, although the older the tree and the faster-growing it is, the greater are the chances that larger knot-free sections are found.

Rays

Depending on the species, rays are the visible streaks that spread horizontally from the center of the trunk to the bark. They transmit food energy inward and outward. They help in identifying some trees, but their main benefit is that in some species, such as the ash, the rays are tightly intermeshed and therefore stitch together a tighter wood, less apt to split, more dense.

Annual Rings

In both the softwoods and hardwoods, such as spruce and birch, the speed of seasonal growth varies. After the winter when sap does not flow, spring loosens the cold grip on trees and sap once again flows, usually comparatively fast at first. In some hardwood maples you can actually see the sap flowing through cracks in the bark when the nights are cold and the days are warm—the perfect maple-sugaring time that lasts about three weeks. Sometimes this fast-flowing sap seeps through the bark and on down the trunk. Gray and red squirrels have a licking feast on these great days.

During this fast, spring, sap-flowing activity, the cambium is extremely active in producing more wood cells. When summer approaches, cambium activity is slowed down as the trees settle in after the rebirth of spring. The cambium then in turn slows down its production of new wood cells.

As a result, when a trunk is cut horizontally the differences between spring and summer wood production is seen as annual rings. The fast spring growth is usually lighter in color and looser in texture. Slower summer growth is usually darker and denser. No new wood is produced in winter, so the following spring growth next to the summer growth shows up on the trunk as lighter and less dense. The continuing effect is a series of rings spreading from the center of the tree. (In the tropics with year-round growing seasons, some species produce nearly ringless trunks.)

Each ring means one year of growth. Counting each ring from the center reveals the age of the tree. Besides that, noticing the difference in the width of individual rings can also indicate whether that year was dry and hot and therefore of little growth, or rainy and cool and of greater growth.

SOFTWOODS

The conifers contain resin as well as generally being composed of softer wood than the broadleaf hardwoods. (Resin in the pine family of trees is a

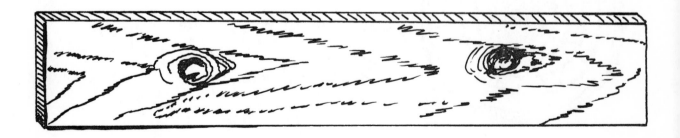

viscous, saplike tarry liquid that is burnable and can increase the heat potential of logs, although the creosote distilled from the wood tar can accumulate in the chimney flue.) The density of the softwoods is less than that of the broadleaf trees and therefore a cord of conifer logs does not hold as much potential heat value by equal measurement with hardwoods.

Generally, the softwoods are the needle-leaf trees that bear their seeds in cones. These include the pines, spruces, hemlocks, cedars, firs, redwoods. They are the evergreens that do not lose their leaves during fall and winter, although in cold climates their growth period stops.

The softwoods have their value in wood heating fuel, especially in industrial and community heating and power plants. In the home, however, care must be used in burning large, continuing quantities of conifers to avoid chimney fires as a result of creosote residue.

HARDWOODS

Most trees are hardwood, a vague term that is useful for not much more than differentiating two of the largest groups of trees in this country. Generally, hardwood trees are just that—harder than the softwoods, but not always. The poplars, classified as a leaf-dropping hardwood, is an exception because its wood is lighter and more porous than some of the softwoods. Don't let the exceptions, however, be more confusing than they deserve.

As a good solid rule, the hardwoods grow in greater density and mass and therefore have more potential, long-lasting heat value per cord because more poundage can be stacked per cord. The hardwoods are easily identified by the extended, thin leaves of innumerable shapes and sizes. They include oak, maple, hickory, ash, birch, willow, elm, aspen, sycamore, and the other flat, wide-leaf trees.

For stoves and fireplaces, one important point to remember is that the hardwoods contain no resin that can cause creosote hazards in the chimney flue. If possible, then, hardwoods should be the first choice over softwoods. Even within the hardwood category, the wide variety of heat potential of certain species per cord and ease of fire maintenance makes knowing the choice of trees worthwhile.

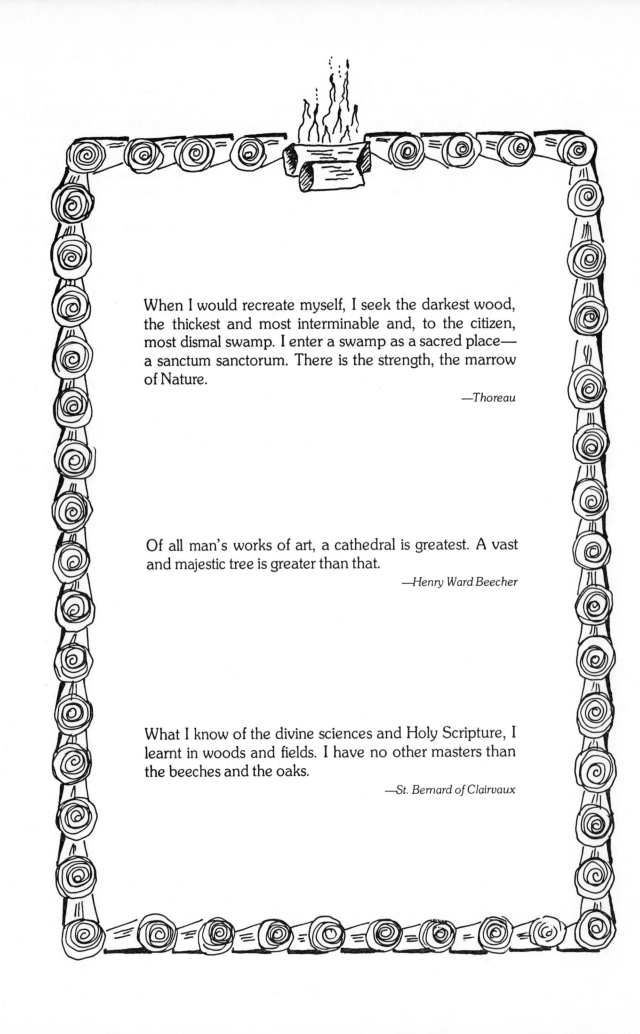

When I would recreate myself, I seek the darkest wood,
the thickest and most interminable and, to the citizen,
most dismal swamp. I enter a swamp as a sacred place—
a sanctum sanctorum. There is the strength, the marrow
of Nature.

—*Thoreau*

Of all man's works of art, a cathedral is greatest. A vast
and majestic tree is greater than that.

—*Henry Ward Beecher*

What I know of the divine sciences and Holy Scripture, I
learnt in woods and fields. I have no other masters than
the beeches and the oaks.

—*St. Bernard of Clairvaux*

Chapter 3

WOOD FUEL

Of all the fuel sources used in the world, wood is the simplest to understand. It is also the one with the least harmful side effects and by-products. And, if that isn't enough to win first place, it has a natural, mesmerizing, peaceful charm about it that anyone who has ever sat in front of a camp fire or fireplace knows about. Even in a closed cast-iron stove, wood fuel instills a primeval security in nearly anyone with any sense of who they are and where they come from. Wood fuel, in other words, keeps us in close touch with our ultimate life-sustaining forces and makes Mother Earth mean something more than a catch phrase.

This directness with the living process is important, but so are economics, convenience, aesthetics, health, and safety of energy sources. Wood fuel does not rate 100 percent better on all these factors. No fuel does, but, overall, burning wood is the most sensible, pleasant way of space heating our homes available now to the mass of Americans.

To be sure, wood heat is not the solution to every single personal or national energy crisis. Yet it can solve far more problems than many people realize. And remember that knowing your way around the main streets of the world of wood eliminates many future home-fire troubles in the process.

WHY WOOD FUEL IN THE FIRST PLACE?

More than any other major fuel, wood provides us with independence. Our own woodpile means if all else fails, if electrical brownouts turn to blackouts, if the Arabs twist off the oil valves, if Washington rations home-heating fuels, we still have a source of heat that does not rely on someone

else to deliver it or on machinery that can suddenly break or leak. In a real sense, we're home free.

When we burn wood, the ash residue can be collected and sprinkled as lime and potash on gardens and lawns; it makes effective fertilizer and in turn leaves nothing behind in the heating process. Every cord of solid hardwood gives up only about 60 pounds of ash, about 1 percent of the total weight of the cord, whereas a ton of coal can leave up to 300 pounds of residue, about 15 percent solid waste per ton.

Minute amounts of sulfur dioxide are released in wood fuel, but in the Number 2 oil that is normally used in home-heating systems nearly all of the .5 percent sulfur it contains is released as sulfur dioxide when oil furnaces are operating. This is an expensive assault against the environment, a long unilateral war against Nature that we are now being forced to pay for in money and overdue bills of responsibility in order to control it.

Not only is wood comparatively pollution-free, it is also an obviously renewable resource. The fossil fuels—oil, gas, and coal—required millennia to decompose and compress into energies; once they are extracted and burned, that's it—no more, gone forever with no chance whatsoever for regeneration. Trees, on the other hand, can be reseeded both by nature and by man. Given proper management, some species such as the eucalyptus can be harvested for fuel within 6 or 7 years. Other woods can be harvested for fuel in 10 or 12 years.

In the meantime, dead branches, diseased limbs, brushwood, and dead trees can be taken for fuel until the replanted tree has expanded its trunk to stove size. This clearing and weeding of a woodlot also allows the principal trees to grow unhampered in more sunlight with less competition and therefore faster.

Unlike the other fuels, wood can be harvested by nearly anyone with careful eye and hand, and unlike the fossil fuels, wood is available in sight and in nearly all types of country. No multimillion-dollar drilling platforms are needed to harvest wood and no PhD degrees are needed to theorize where the oaks and maples are located. So wood fuel is relatively inexpensive to harvest.

Wood fuel can also better heat individual rooms with better control. In fact, with wood and a little bit of skill it's possible to keep log consumption down with a very low fire at certain times of the day and night.

If you only even partly fuel your home with wood, the advantages far outweigh the disadvantages. Wood does take more space to store; it does get messy; it does take work input; and it does require periodical attention. Yet the exercise of gathering your own fuel, the comfort and pride of seeing your work stacked and ready to fire, and the direct control you have over your own heating fuel gives you a sense of self-reliance you never had before. It also makes you realize how sensible it is in the first place.

THE HEAT IN TREES

As a solar collector, a tree is highly efficient. Through photosynthesis, it stores the chemical energy of the sun in great living quantities, never diminishing its potential, always increasing it. When that energy from the sun is unlocked by a match, the heat in the tree is sunlight in your stove.

Every tree has the same amount of heat energy in it pound for pound—approximately 8,600 British Thermal Units. (BTUs are the universal measuring base to compare differences in heat output; one BTU raises the temperature of one pound of water one degree Fahrenheit. One BTU is, in everyday language, the approximate equivalent to the heat in one kitchen match.)

If we discount resin, the pure wood in the logs from a birch, a pine, an elm, a spruce contain the same heat potential. All wood—twigs, branches, and trunks—contains the same 8,600 BTUs pound for pound.

The key to selecting different species of trees available to you is remembering this figure in relationship to the fact that different species have different densities. It follows that if oak has more wood heat potential packed into a tighter mass than poplar, then oak has more heat concentrated in less space. Therefore, pound for pound the BTU potential is the same for all wood, but cord for cord it is not. More oak wood can be packed into a cord than can poplar wood. As a result, a cord of oak can provide more heat than a cord of poplar. If the price of a cord of oak and of poplar is the same, the choice of oak on a purely BTU/dollar-bill equation is obvious.

The standard cord by which laboratory tests are made is a stack of wood 4 feet by 4 feet by 8 feet, or 128 cubic feet. However, the air space between the logs generally accounts for 50 cubic feet or so. The amount of solid wood in a cord is generally considered to be between 75 and 85 cubic feet.

Since all species produce the same 8,600 BTUs per pound and since all species have different densities, the following table shows how denser wood produces more heat in one air-dried cord of wood:

Wood	Weight per Cord	BTUs in Millions
Ash	3,440	20.0
Aspen	2,160	12.5
Beech, American	3,760	21.8
Birch, yellow	3,680	21.3
Elm, American	2,900	17.2
Hickory, shagbark	4,240	24.6
Maple, red	3,200	18.6
Maple, sugar	3,680	21.3
Oak, red	3,680	21.3
Oak, white	3,920	22.7
Pine, eastern white	2,080	13.3

In general, the hardwood trees release twice as much heat as the softwoods. For example, the broadleaf shagbark hickory and the needle-leaf

Oil   140,000 BTUs/gal.
Gas   1,000 BTUs/cu. ft.

EQUIVALENT TO ONE CORD OF WOOD AIR-DRIED

Wood	Coal (tons)	Oil (gal.)	Gas (100 cu. ft.)
Ash	1.10	145	251
Aspen	.69	91	158
Beech, American	1.20	158	274
Birch, yellow	1.18	154	268
Elm, American	.93	125	211
Hickory, shagbark	1.36	178	309
Maple, red	1.02	135	233
Maple, sugar	1.18	154	268
Oak, red	1.18	154	268
Oak, white	1.26	165	286
Pine, eastern white	.67	96	152

By combining the BTU figures with the oil equivalent figures, you can equate one cord of red oak (21,300,000 BTUs) with 154 gallons of Number 2 fuel oil, or any other combination that might lock into an easy equation to keep in mind.

Unfortunately, not every BTU is delivered into your home for heat when the wood is burned. It

eastern white pine in the preceding table have weight and BTU values very close to double, or half of, each other. If the resin in most softwoods is discounted (resin itself produces twice as much heat by weight than wood) and the moisture content is at the air-dried level of the stable 15 to 20 percent, one cord of hardwood produces approximately the equivalent of one ton of coal. This is easy to remember and can clear up the BTU mystery: one cord of hardwood equals one ton of coal.

A cord of hickory or maple or elm or beech all equal one ton of heat value of coal. At the other end of this general scale, *two* cords of softwood cedar or spruce or cypress or white pine equals one ton of coal in BTU potential. In between, according to tests made by the U.S. Forest Products Laboratory in Madison, Wisconsin, 1.5 cords of sycamore or western hemlock or Douglas fir equal one ton of coal.

The following two tables show the equivalent BTU values of wood relative to coal, oil, and gas:

Wood   8,600 BTUs/lb.
Coal   11,000 BTUs/lb.

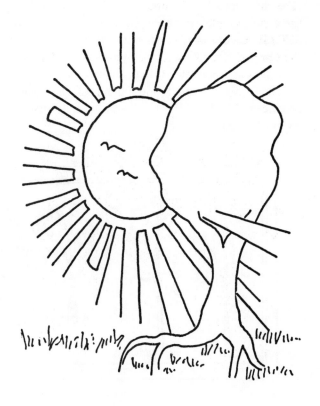

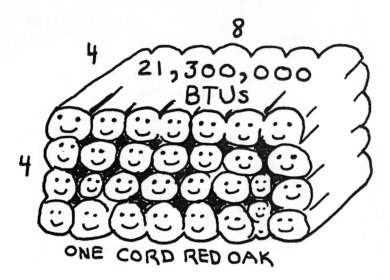

takes heat merely to evaporate the moisture left in the wood, in a sense robbing heat from itself. About 1,000 BTUs are needed per pound of wood to raise the temperature to evaporation point (212 degrees) as well as another 350 BTUs that carry the steam up the flue. So in effect one pound of dry wood produces 7,250 BTUs that are actually usable energy for space heating.

REBIRTH OF WOOD POWER

Unlocking the solar energy in trees was the main source of power that laid the foundation of industrial America. Wood provided up to 90 percent of the energy expended in this country until the middle of the nineteenth century. When the railroads and heavy steel and iron industries

developed, wood was gradually replaced as the primary fuel. By 1885 coal became the principal fuel source. By 1910 wood accounted for only 10 percent of the national energy needs. Coal continued to be increasingly the chief fuel, that is, until cheap oil and gas took over three decades later.

Today the fossil fuel gap in history is closing its mortgage and we're once again looking to wood power. The expense of petroleum, now the dominant fuel, along with its eventual depletion, our continuing dependence on its foreign supply, our monumental loss of capital to it, and, not the least, the havoc petroleum and its by-products have wreaked on the land and water make the alternative energy of wood once again feasible in many large- and small-scale needs.

Burning wood for specialized industry exists today, especially in the Pacific Northwest, but scientists are now proposing and experimenting with wood-fueled power plants for entire communities. The costs are competitive with petroleum-based electrical power plants and, as the cost of mining uranium rises, with nuclear plants as well.

George Szego, energy specialist and president of the InterTechnology Corporation in Warrenton, Virginia, proposes that trees be planted, harvested, and burned in converted conventional power plants to produce industrial and residential electricity. Wood fuel, he calculates, would burn at 40 percent efficiency and could be reharvested every 10 years. No fossil fuel can match this valuable potential.

The Green Mountain Power Company in Vermont is experimenting with a small wood-fired community power plant in Milton, Vermont, a community of 4,000. The oil-based plant would be converted to wood power.

Robert Thompson, president of Environment, Inc., of Guilford, Connecticut, has prepared feasibility studies for this project and urges the conversion. He finds that the annual savings by burning wood instead of oil would be $840,000, more than half the cost of the oil bill.

Cost factors are based on the stable inherent potential of 8,600 BTUs in every pound of wood, no matter what kind. Thompson calculates that the cost of fuel could be reduced by half, in addition to eliminating the need to buy 152 million barrels of oil for the Milton generating plant.

The kicker is that, given the nature of wood energy potential, any parts of trees can be burned for the same fuel capability. In other words, using wood for power does not in any way interfere with any other timbering operation. No prime lumber needs to be used for fuel, no logs destined for shiny tables and chairs or wall facings. Instead, branches, dead trees, scrub brush, any low-grade cull wood will do.

In fact, using wood for fuel on a large-scale industrial basis would benefit the image and efficiency of the timber industry. The U.S. Department of Agriculture states that only 60 percent of any tree harvested for consumer use results in a product. The other 40 percent is wasted. This is like taking 10 years to build a 10-room house, occupying 6 rooms, and demolishing the other 4 rooms. It doesn't make any sense. The lumber mills are not interested in stumps, barks, and branches, but those looking to redevelop wood power are.

Since most forest waste wood is either piled,

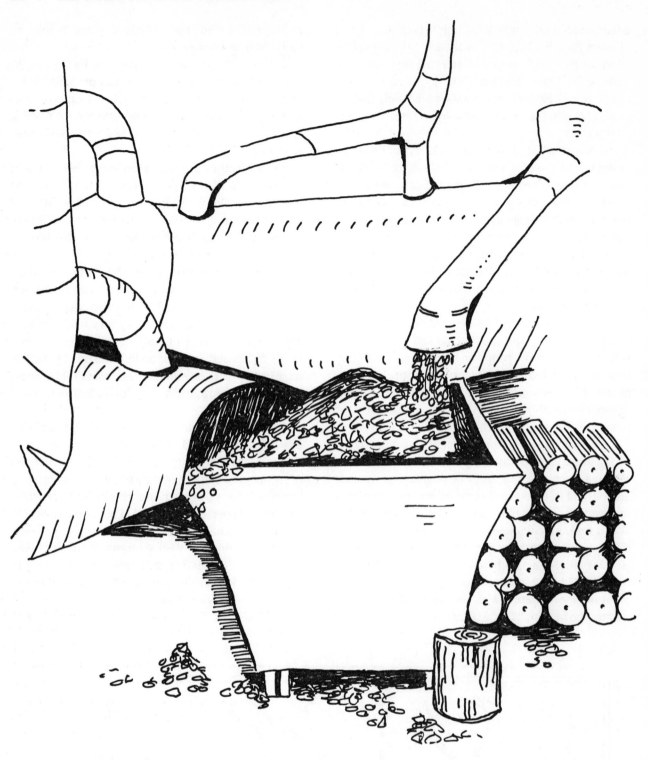

left to rot, or uselessly burned to get rid of it, a major source of energy is waiting to be tapped. The conservative estimate of 6.6 billion board feet of waste wood generated every year equals one half the current annual consumption of forest products.

One of the companies that is doing something about taking advantage of this smoldering wood power is Forest Fuels of Keene, New Hampshire. Robert Caughey, a consulting chemical engineer and machine designer for Weyerhaeuser, Boise

Cascade, and other major companies, has developed a wood-chip gas burner now operating as a space heater for a lumber mill and kiln drying oven in Alstead, New Hampshire.

The burner works this way: Outside the room containing the reconverted oil burner, a bin designed to hold 36 hours of wood-chip heat is loaded by a tractor scoop. The green wet waste wood chips are fed slowly and automatically by conveyor belt into an enclosed sheet metal channel where waste stack heat is recirculated to dry the chips (one inch long, a quarter of an inch thick) to about 4 percent moisture content. The continuing process takes 40 minutes from green chips to dry. The dry chips are then fed by an enclosed turn screw through the building wall to the burner into which the chips drop steadily between two grates. There in the firebox the chips burn to release their gas and heat, which reaches 1,200 degrees. The burning carbon monoxide in the adjacent boiler reaches 2,200 degrees, depending on the oxygen supply. The firebox normally burns about 200 pounds of chips an hour, but can handle 300 pounds an hour, the equivalent to 2.5 million BTUs or 100 horsepower. The beauty of it is the simplicity.

Caughey is convinced that the use of wood can make a substantial impact on the energy crisis. Since any kind of wood yields the same amount of heat per pound, any kind of wood, dead or alive, can be used in Caughey's burner. "One ton of dry wood will provide more heat than 100 gallons of oil," he said. "Actually, 100 gallons of oil will produce about 14 million BTUs and one ton of dry wood will produce about 17 million BTUs. We can use any old dirty chips, dead bark, dead wood, any species. So far as BTUs are concerned, it's immaterial."

John Calhoun, consulting forester and president of Forest Fuels, said the principle behind their wood-gas burner is an old one. Such burners were used during World War II before gas and oil became inexpensive and readily available.

Now that he and Caughey have industrial burners operating efficiently, they're designing and marketing wood burners for home use. Wood chips (eventually to be pelletized for standard weight and size) would be fed automatically into a home burner. This would be easier and more efficient than burning cordwood. He also estimates that home owners would pay between $7 and $25 a ton

for wood chips that would produce the same amount of heat as 100 gallons of oil costing $40 to $46.

Contrary to popular belief, Americans use less wood today than they did 100 years ago. In the mid-nineteenth century families were burning up to 17 cords a year for overall household use. Even with the advent of chemical wood processing to manufacture commercial products, the harvest of our forests is far less than at the turn of the century when close to 17 billion board feet were cut. Today about 12 billion board feet are harvested, nearly half ending up as waste. With industrial and home wood burners now operating and spreading, that waste wood no longer needs to be wasted.

HARDWOODS OR SOFTWOODS?

For stoves and fireplaces the choice is not simply between one or the other. If both general species were readily available, which is usually not the case (approximately 90 percent of the hardwoods grow in the East), selecting the hardwoods every time over softwoods doesn't necessarily fit every fire need.

Sometimes you may want a quick, hot, short fire to lessen morning chill in the house before you leave for the day. Other times you may spend the entire weekend at home and therefore want slow-burning, trouble-free heat. In the first instance, softwood is preferable; in the second, hardwood.

The prevailing experience is that softwood provides quick-starting, high-heat fires. Hardwoods provide longer-lasting, more uniform fires. Some old hands at fire-building, like the sourdoughs of Alaska, keep softwood kindling and small sticks together with larger hardwood logs. That way they can reach a hot flame quickly with the softwood so the hardwood can catch and burn to a faster coal stage for long-term heat. One ideal fire-making, fire-sustaining combination would be to use any kind of cedar for kindling and follow it up with oak or beech.

Softwoods contain about 15 percent resin, which is highly flammable. It also generates creosote soot in the chimney flue—the reason too much softwood burning is not good nor as safe as the dense, resin-free woods.

If you're looking eventually for an even-burning, red-hot fire that puts out a lot of heat without your having constantly to add logs to it, then the hardwood oaks, maples, and beeches should be your choice. As a general rule, remember that the denser woods contain more potential heat per log. Hickory, therefore, contains far more heat value than spruce.

Within each of the hardwood and softwood categories lie many variables. A good fire is not merely quick-starting or long-lasting. Different woods have different flame heights and intensities, different tendencies to smoke, different temperaments in sparking. Most hardwoods do not spark, for example, but yellow poplar, a broadleaf hardwood, does. Most softwoods have moderate usable heat value per pound, but the needle-leaf Douglas fir has high heat value. The exceptions are still exceptions, but it proves the point that the choice is not all that automatic.

The following table breaks down these different values of some woods that might be available in your area:

HARDWOODS

Wood	Heat Value	Heavy Smoke	Sparks
Ash, red oak, white oak, beech, hickory, hard maple, pecan, dogwood	High	No	No
Soft maple, cherry, walnut	Medium	No	No
Elm, sycamore, gum	Medium	Medium	No
Aspen, basswood, cottonwood	Low	Medium	No
Chestnut, yellow poplar	Low	Medium	Yes

SOFTWOODS

Wood	Heat Value	Heavy Smoke	Sparks
Southern yellow pine, Douglas fir	High	Yes	No
Cypress, redwood	Medium	Medium	No
White cedar, western red cedar, eastern red cedar	Medium	Medium	Yes
Eastern white pine, western white pine, sugar pine, ponderosa pine, true firs	Low	Medium	No
Tamarack, larch	Medium	Medium	Yes
Spruce	Low	Medium	Yes

ERSATZ LOGS

Supermarket packages of logs are marketed like any other shelf product. Each log is usually individually wrapped in brown paper and costs a high price. Inside isn't really a log, however. It's a cylinder of compressed sawdust treated with paraffin for easy igniting. These far-removed tree products are sometimes further treated with chemicals so that on burning they emit odors ranging from apples to incense. Some are further treated to produce fully green flames or blue or fire-engine red.

One brand is Duraflame, 6 pounds of compressed cedar sawdust, wax, and coloring agent. The "log" is claimed to last 3 hours and produce 90,000 BTUs. As with Sterno Log and other such products selling for about $1.00 a log, these manufactured logs must not be burned in

sheet-metal stoves, cast-iron potbelly stoves, at barbecues, or used for cooking. Only one at a time must be burned and that one must never be broken up or added to an existing fire. In other words, **be careful**. Have nothing to do with it, once it's lighted, or the wax fire may spread. The official warning is: "Use of fire tongs or poker could be hazardous." That about says it.

In a tight pinch these substitute logs can be useful for a sense of fireplace cheer if real logs can't be found or you want to do away with what may be considered the bother of fire-building. They also can be used in conjunction with real logs as ersatz matches to get the real stuff burning, but that makes for expensive matches—and caution.

For whatever reason they are used, manufactured logs are still ground up compressed forest residue. They are not true logs and because of that they will not generate concentrated high heat or coals. In short, for space heating they are virtually useless.

The same is true for homemade newspaper logs. True, newsprint is a wood product, but the density of rolled-up newspaper logs nowhere matches that of a living oak, maple, or pine, for that matter. Even with hand-cranking machines you can use in your basement to get rid of last month's Sunday editions, newspaper logs may be good for a little easy cheer but certainly not for heating your living room or bedroom. You just can't roll them tightly enough.

If you want to try, however, here's one method. Soak newspaper sections overnight in a light soapy solution in a bathtub. Roll the sections tightly onto a wooden pole or rake hoe or broomstick. Remove from the pole and stand them on end. Dry them thoroughly for a couple of weeks. Then put them in the fireplace and pretend.

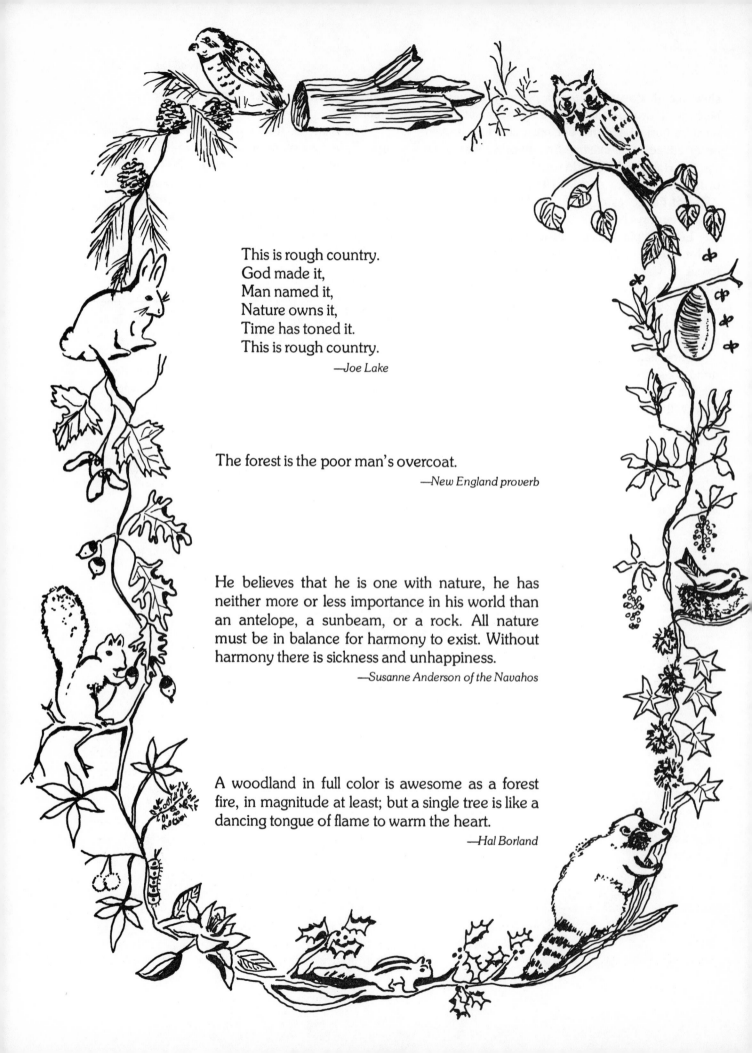

This is rough country.
God made it,
Man named it,
Nature owns it,
Time has toned it.
This is rough country.

—*Joe Lake*

The forest is the poor man's overcoat.

—*New England proverb*

He believes that he is one with nature, he has neither more or less importance in his world than an antelope, a sunbeam, or a rock. All nature must be in balance for harmony to exist. Without harmony there is sickness and unhappiness.

—*Susanne Anderson of the Navahos*

A woodland in full color is awesome as a forest fire, in magnitude at least; but a single tree is like a dancing tongue of flame to warm the heart.

—*Hal Borland*

Chapter 4

GETTING READY

Heating your home doesn't begin with striking a match and touching it to the kindling. It begins with knowing which woods to choose, where to get the best deal on cordwood, convenient ways to stack logs you buck up yourself, how long to season them and why. The more of the right preparation you have behind you, the easier is lighting the fire and keeping it lighted. And that's the core of it all.

SOURCES OF FREE FUEL WOOD

Trees are nearly everywhere, but chopping down your neighbor's elm for your own stove isn't recommended. Finding stove wood is easier than you might expect. When your mental antennae are attuned to searching for wood, many more sources exist than you would think otherwise.

The 1973–74 petroleum crisis, as one example, has opened up fuel-wood supplies accessible to the vast majority of the American population. Since the Arabs tightened their oil faucet, the U.S. Forest Service has conducted a do-it-yourself wood fuel program in the national forests. Many local agencies have done likewise with state forests. The forests, after all, are owned by the public, which is all of us collectively.

Any individual may get a permit to cut and take wood for personal use. All that is required is that the wood must be taken from dead or fallen timber and must not be used for commercial purposes—two simple, sensible rules that anyone can follow. With 150 national forests in 44 states, the proximity of just these sources brings free stove wood close to home for millions of people. When state forests that conduct similar programs are included, the possibilities are even broader. The cost for taking this unwanted timber is usually between only $1 and $3 a cord, practically free. The agencies provide the forest. You provide the handsaw or chain saw, hauling muscle power, and truck or car

for taking the logs home. The Massachusetts "Cut-A-Cord Program" conducted in five state forests is typical of the basic set-up of low charge and open invitation of other programs around the country.

An often overlooked source is as nearby as your town dump. With most town, city, and metropolitan areas now banning backyard trash-burning and large-scale construction burning, the dump is an excellent source of both logs and discarded construction lumber, which can give you fast fires at no cost except the effort of sawing the planks to stove size. Some of the discarded lumber

may generate sparks and creosote, so be judicious in the selection. Nevertheless, the U.S. Forest Service estimates that up to 30 percent of all the trash in a typical town dump is burnable wood.

Going directly to construction sites is often valuable. Contractors are usually very willing to let you haul away their waste wood that you can burn at home. It saves them the trouble of taking it to the dump themselves. You can also follow telephone clearings through the woods after the tree trimmers cut back growth from the wires. New power-line sections are prize sources of raw wood, as are new

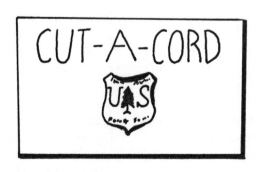

road-construction or street-widening sections that have trees to be cleared. Some crews will cut tree trunks to manageable size for you personally.

Committed wood scavengers make periodic trips to sawmills for slab scraps and other waste material suitable for home burning. Driving around town after a severe wind or ice storm can locate for you fallen trees that homeowners or businesses are more than willing to have somebody clear away right then and there. Making long-distance trips into finished logging areas can reap good supplies of very acceptable stove wood that was very unacceptable for commercial lumber.

City, county, and state forest agents can give you tips on free firewood sources in your local area. All it takes is a telephone call.

Remember, however, to ask permission of the owner of the land or business in all cases. Otherwise, the free wood may not be so free. Most counties and states have specific laws that prohibit the destroying or taking of trees, shrubs, and vines on both private and public property. The laws carry with the infringements either fines, imprisonment, or even the loss of a driving license. Unless the owner uses his woods for his own fuel supply, chances are that asking permission ends up being little more than a courtesy. If not, explain to him that weeding a forest in the long run produces a faster-growing, healthier stock of trees just as weeding out the weak, leaching plants does for a vegetable garden.

BUYING CORDWOOD

In the old days when families that depended entirely on wood to heat their homes and cook their meals had to buy it, getting exactly what they paid for was important. They made it their business to know their woods and to know exactly what constituted a full cord. Paying the same amount of money for hemlock as for dogwood was out of the question since the heat value per cord was nowhere near the same. In the same way, being short-measured on the size of a cord was never overlooked by anyone in those days when money was scarce and alternate fuels didn't exist.

Today state agents don't measure stacks of wood with regulation lengths of string, or cords (hence the name). They aren't around dealers to make sure that the common customer is getting a fair shake. Unless buyers can rely on known reputable fuel-wood suppliers, it's good to be prepared to cast a critical eye on any cordwood you need to buy.

The price of a cord of mixed hardwoods a century ago was between $2 and $8. That price went down to $1 when coal, oil, and gas prevailed around the Depression years. Nowadays the price of a cord varies anywhere from $25 in the country to $100 a cord in the city, as it did in Boston last winter.

Unfortunately, the modern price was and is still being paid by customers not wary or informed enough about what they are purchasing. When customers pay inflated prices for less than they expect they're getting, it adds up to a thriving profitable business, especially when more than 16 million cords of wood are consumed throughout the country every year. With the continuing energy crisis, the total will rise, it's estimated, to 18 million cords in the next four years.

Traditionally, a cord is a neatly stacked compact rectangle of logs measuring 4 feet by 4 feet by 8 feet. If the logs are split, more wood is usually included in this 128-cubic-feet area. Over the years the word *cord* has been too loosely referred to in

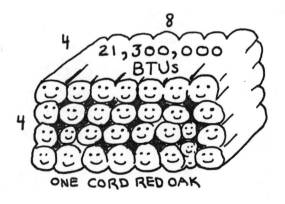

ONE CORD RED OAK

other measurements. Terms such as face cord, stove-wood cord, running cord become confusing if the exact measurements of a full cord aren't kept in mind.

Since most people burn logs in relatively small stoves and fireplaces, suppliers sell cords with logs 16 inches or 18 inches in length. The 4-foot height and 8-foot length of the cord is the same, but this face cord is only about a third to a half of a full cord, depending on the log length not cut to the standard 4 feet. Buyers should keep these critical measurements in mind and the price quoted for both a full cord and a face cord.

When you buy a cord and can have the logs cut to size, measure the smallest width of your fireplace grate or the shortest length of your stove and have the dealer cut according to this number. Pay accordingly.

Full cord:	4' by 4' by 8'
Half cord:	2' by 4' by 8'
Third cord:	16'' by 4' by 8'
Quarter cord:	12'' by 4' by 8'

Some buyers have difficulty distinguishing green or partially green wood from dry wood. Be aware that some dealers would be pleased to get green wood out of the way so that it doesn't take up room for seasoning. If you're not sure whether or not the wood is green, let it air-dry for five or six months before burning it. That'll ease your mind about making good fires as well as not clogging up your chimney flue with tars.

If you buy wood by the ton, it's especially important to distinguish between green and dry wood. Some woods have nearly equal weights of water as wood. Most newly cut trees contain 50 to 60 percent moisture content. Totaled in a cord this can amount to half a ton of water per ton of wood. If you bought the cord of green wood, you bought a lot of water you can't drink. Don't buy by the ton if you can avoid it.

Buy by the cord. That way you can see if the wood is split and stacked tightly in an area you can measure yourself, no matter what size it is. If all you can buy is green wood and you and the buyer know it, then ask that an extra layer of small logs be put on top to compensate for the moisture that will evaporate as you season the wood.

YOUR OWN WOODLOT

Managing your own wood fuel sees you through from start to finish. Many private landowners have wood acreage that is not only being wasted but is also less productive simply because it is not being managed. Whether you have your own woodlot or not, count those people lucky who can guide the growth of their trees, improve the growing rate by selective weeding, cut their own stove wood, buck it up into their own logs, and burn the

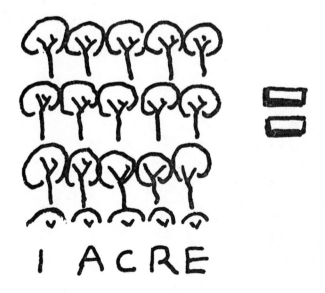

1 ACRE

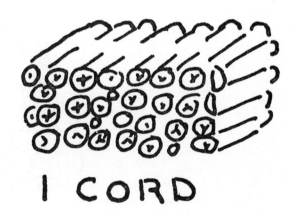

1 CORD

fuel they raised and nurtured themselves. It's a nice feeling to be as energy self-reliant as this.

Robert Caughey of Forest Fuels, for one, cut his oil bill in half one winter by merely going out on his six acres and collecting dead branches and limbs and burning them. "I didn't cut a live tree," he said, "and I've been doing this for four years."

Ecologists have calculated that, with all factors being equal, one acre can provide one cord of wood in one year. Automatically. No replanting necessary; no secret formulas applied. One acre, one cord, one year.

How many cords of wood are needed for a winter depends on where you live, wind protection, how well your house is insulated, how large your house is, and other similar considerations. As an old-time rule, cold Maine winters were said to require 15 cords to live in splendor. The more generally accepted rule of thumb now is that for an average-size six-room house about seven cords are adequate for full-time heating in cold climates. Too many ingredients, such as how well you build and maintain your fires, how well the heat is distributed in your house, and what kind of stove you're using, enter in to figure exactly. Seven cords, however, work for the average and can be adjusted to individual situations.

If that's what it takes, then seven acres of woodlot could provide seven cords of stove wood without depleting the source in any way. In less severe climates, smaller woodlots would do the same job.

Basic management of a woodlot involves thinning the stand as well as weeding out diseased and dead trees. The dead trees are easily recognized, but improvement cutting takes a more discerning eye. For this you must first decide what trees you wish to let stand and then decide what the stand will look like after you cut away the weed trees.

For instance, if a tree has spread its canopy over a group of struggling young hardwoods, that dominating tree may have to go. It is blocking valuable sunlight from the younger trees and hindering their growth. Groups of trees squashed together likewise must be thinned because the competition for nutrients, sunlight, and water is making them crowd into each other; they all lose in their potential growth. So does your future wood supply.

A good woodlot should have shafts of sunlight streaking through to the forest floor. It should be airy and free of scrub brush. It should have a thriving combination of seedlings, saplings, and full-grown species. Above all, it should show signs of attention and care.

Since the high cost of a cord bought from a dealer results from nearly 100 percent labor cost, managing your own woodlot can reap 100 percent profits. The trees cost nothing to grow. As for your own labor, well, consider it good healthy times in the outdoors.

FELLING YOUR FUEL

Cutting your own stove wood is hard work, but getting out in the fresh air, walking over the forest floor, smelling the pungency of mosses and wild wintergreen and white birches, selecting your future heat source, smelling the lightness of the sawdust, and hearing the tree creak and crack and finally fall with the thump that means even more hard work to come is all worth the effort.

Nevertheless, anyone who has done it knows that the effort is none too slight. Later on, when you place the logs in your stove or fireplace, you appreciate, you treasure, every flickering flame they produce, but at the time of gathering your wood stock it pays to look ahead.

The key to keeping the work to a minimum is to pick your site and arrange your car or truck or horse (whichever is the best way) for transporting the logs so that the number of times you handle the wood is the smallest possible. Every situation is different, but experienced hands find that if you have to touch

the wood in the entire process a total of five or six times, or carry it more than 10 feet, you're making work for yourself.

A long-handled poleax is one of the traditional, solid tools of the forest. This old method of harvesting trees is invigorating and relatively quiet. Axing trees, however, can be dangerous for the inexperienced. If you're one of them, ease into the swing of things.

A hatchet can be handy for lopping off twigs and small branches, but this one-handed ax is probably one of the most dangerous tools around. Use it with extreme care. Many a knee and shinbone have been damaged as the blade head slipped, ricocheted, or reverberated from a hardy swing.

For sheer muscle power the one- or two-person bow saw is the most satisfying way of cutting stove wood. A good sturdy bow with a curved tube handle connecting both ends of the blade usually costs between $5 and $10. Bow saws are extremely versatile and effective. If two people are using one, the best way for each person to work it is to pull one way but do not push the other. In other words, each person pulls back, in turn, thereby splitting the sawing effort in two.

If winter is too difficult a time in which to work, summer and late fall are good seasons for cutting wood. In summer when you fell a tree leave it lying as is for two or three weeks. During this time the leaves still attached will evaporate some of the moisture in the wood and lessen the seasoning time after you buck it up. This wood can be used the following spring, if your winter supply is fading or,

better yet, the following winter. Late fall has most of the broad leaves off the tree and the weather is crisp and invigorating. Since cutting timber boils up a steam, the cooler weather makes the work tolerable, if not easier.

A rough eye measurement of how much wood is on the stump is that a tree 20 inches in diameter at chest height probably has close to a cord in it.

Chain-sawing is the speediest, most time-efficient method for felling a tree. It is also the godawful noisiest (wear ear guards if you're sawing more than 10 minutes) and can be body-ripping as well. Unless you have a huge chunk stove, you'll seldom drop a 36-inch-diameter oak, so don't buy the largest size chain saw on the market shelf. The smaller models in the 10-inch or 12-inch class are completely adequate for nearly any job worth spending time on. They're also far easier to handle. A 10-inch guide bar doesn't restrict you to 10-inch-diameter tree trunks, either. You can handle larger trunks by cutting both sides in turn.

Whatever you do, keep the chain saw in perfect condition. Lubricate it, keep it sharp, follow the manufacturer's instructions to the letter, and, above all, keep your mind on your job. Too many people have ended up chain-sawing their leg bones to near disaster. Don't let it happen to you.

Using a chain saw to fell a tree starts with carefully inspecting the lay of the land and the surrounding trees. If the forest is fairly thick, a fall path should be partially cleared so that the tree doesn't get strung up on the tangle of other branches, which it can easily do. If it does, you have further and

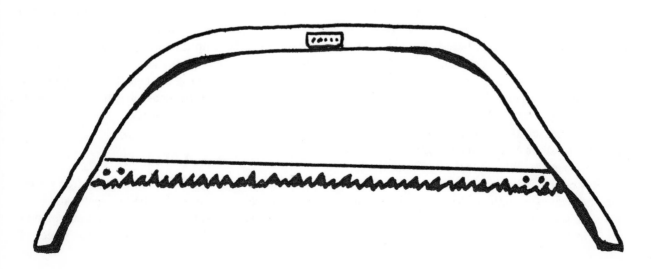

more risky problems in getting it to the ground by sawing progressively from the bottom of the trunk upward, letting the tree fall more and more by its own collapse of the supporting angle.

If you have a block and tackle or a good 100-foot rope, tie one or the other as high as you can climb the ladder you have with you or the tree itself. How the tightened rope is angled to help guide the tree down the clearing depends on your judgment of how the tree will fall.

Experienced hands can readily judge in what direction a heavy tree will fall. Beginners can only guess at the weight balance of the tree in relationship to the flatness or tilt of the land. Beginners then should be extremely careful to keep completely clear of the front and side angles of the fall.

Cutting the upright tree is relatively straightforward business. The first cut is on the side of the direction you want the tree to fall. Cut one third to one half of the distance straight into the trunk. Cut the downward angle to meet the first cut and then remove the wedge of wood. At the back side of the trunk cut straight to the center of the tree on a level with the bottom of the wedge cut. The weight of the tree may lean it back and pinch the saw. If it does, insert an iron wedge to keep the tree weight off the saw. Continue the cut until the tree falls. Be aware that sometimes a tree will, as it falls, slip its trunk back. Keep your chin out of the way.

BUCKING

Once the tree is on the ground, you have to decide whether to buck it up to stove-wood lengths or merely to cut it to convenient transportation lengths to take back to your woodshed. (The third alternative is simply to leave cord-size logs in the woods to season. But that depends on where you are.) The decision is largely based on what kind of hauling rig you have. You can't get four-foot lengths into ordinary cars, but you can in station wagons and you can in pickup trucks.

Most people who cut their own wood prefer to take the longer lengths back home where they can saw them to stove size at their own convenience when time permits. Whatever the decision, the tree must now be sheared of its smallest branches first to clear the way for cutting the larger limbs and trunks. This again is all straightforward business. It does help to clear away the smaller branches as

they fall so you won't trip over them while you're chain-sawing the larger ones.

If the tree is not flat on solid ground, try to brace it up with any kind of wedge invention so that it doesn't sag and pinch your saw as you work. If you're cutting to stove size and want the logs as uniform in length as possible, measure a stick or knot a string to the proper size, 16 inches or 18 inches or 24 inches or whatever, and mark with an ax, hatchet, or handsaw along the trunk and branches sections in that length. Then you can zip from one section to the other and chain-saw right away without measuring each time.

Likewise, if you use a sawhorse to buck up smaller logs by hand, use one that doesn't force you to bend your back too much. Also, with a six-leg sawhorse to hold up the end of the log you're sawing to size, you can mark the exact stove length you want without having it tilt and fall and make you swear. It speeds up the measuring and standardizes your logs for future convenience.

SPLITTING

Once you get the swing of it, most tree woods are relatively easy to split. The few really stubborn ones are sycamore, black gum, and red gum. Don't even bother with the elm, the stubbornest queen of

all. Chain-saw it. You'll save yourself time and consternation. It's the reason elm makes good ax handles.

To split wood effectively, set up a system that keeps your movements to a minimum and establishes a smooth, easygoing rhythm. You can split wood decently enough on a base of Mother Earth herself, but if it's soft ground the impact is dissipated and splitting the wood either takes more muscle or more time. It's better to place the wood you want to split on a wide solid plank board, another bigger, wider circle of wood, or in a felled tree crotch.

A strong overhead swing of an ax to the center of a comparatively small chunk of wood or to one third of a larger piece will, after some practice, do the job with a single try. Splitting wood this way is one of the old-time arts.

Using a sledgehammer and a steel wedge may be less dramatic but it's just as effective. Sometimes it may take longer; other times it works with a single swing as the ax does. With a hammer and wedge, powerful strokes aren't necessary—something to think about if a lot of wood needs to be split in one afternoon—and you're not in Paul Bunyan shape.

To do so, simply tap the wedge into the wood where you want it to split. Then either one strong blow or repeated easier blows on the wedge pries the wood apart. If you have to, you can merely keep hammering the wedge all the way through the separating wood. No failures in this method. It's surefire.

Knots in wood are virtually unsplittable. Forget about whacking through them. Either chip around them, chain-saw them, or burn the whole chunk if you can.

Splitting wood is one of the traditional good feelings that come from preparing your wood fuel. This is the step that gets closer to the heart of the entire wood power process. With simple tools and simple movements, you crack open the treasure boxes that are going to keep you warm and make you feel in close touch with the forces that are important to an earthbound life. The thud and the split jolt right through your hands and arms and back. You feel it in your muscles, but you feel it in your soul, too.

STACKING

A well-stacked supply of cordwood is the mark of someone who is both efficient and has an eye for the beautiful. A symmetrical, even, varied-size bank of logs is a sight few people tire of—certainly not the people who made the stack.

A stack of wood is not a pile of wood. Even if

the stack is in pyramid shape, there is always a method to it. Stacking does take the shape of the container, if one is used, such as a woodshed or garage or back porch. Otherwise, the shape is up to the stacker. It makes no difference so long as it is in the open air and keeps the logs handy.

One unusual shape is called the beehive. Larger stumps are placed and stacked in a circle, the smaller logs heaped on them, and the twigs and branches put on the very top. A rounded, symmetrical, conical shape keeps all from falling apart and makes such a stack a conversation piece as well as effectively keeping different sizes of wood together for long-term seasoning.

Another method of stacking in the open is to design braces to hold the logs. All it takes is forking some sticks or planks against both ends of the stack as it builds up. An easier, although not always convenient, method is simply to stack logs between two growing trees. That eliminates the need to make the braces. Using upright trees for the job is sensible and probably the most popular method for field drying.

Whatever the shape and container, wood should be stacked on runner poles or plank board. This raises the wood from the soil and prevents rotting of the entire bottom layer of logs. Rotten sections of logs contain extremely little heat value.

Split wood should be stacked with the bark side up to act as a shield against rain and melting snow. If the stack is all exposed to the elements, a heavy-gauge plastic sheet should be placed over the top,

weighted, and let hung down partly over the sides, also to shield against rain and snow.

A good solid way to brace the stack is to crisscross both end layers of logs. This method is far sturdier than stacking the logs all in the same direction—a system that with one key log removed can send an avalanche of heavy wood over your feet.

If wood is stacked thoughtfully and consistently, little chance follows that it will fall either way. It's also a good idea to keep the stack no higher than your shoulders. It may be easy to throw a log up on a six and a half foot high stack, but removing the top layers later on is awkward and trouble-born.

SEASONING

Drying the split logs in the open air reduces the moisture content of wood to about a stable 20 percent. Generally, the smaller and shorter the logs, the quicker the seasoning process. The water content mostly draws out lengthwise in the logs, so a woodshed with only a roof that allows circulation of air on both sides of the stack is more effective.

For most woods seasoning is needed in order to produce good steady fires. In the South, wood should be air-dried for three months; in the North, six months at the minimum, preferably a year. The gain in heat potential is figured at 6.7 percent when wood reduces its moisture content from 60 to 20 percent. Three months of seasoning reduces the moisture content to 35 percent, still not enough for smooth-burning fires. For home stoves and fireplaces seasoning is essential.

If wood is not seasoned before being burned, the moisture and resin trapped inside the wood cells build up pressure from the heat and explode as sparks. This makes for unpleasant and sometimes unsafe fires.

When green wood is burned, approximately one seventh of its heat value is drained off by the need of the fire to heat the moisture so that the water will dissipate. Green wood is 10 to 44 percent less efficient as a heater than air-dried wood.

The figures tell the advantages of seasoned wood:

MOISTURE CONTENT

Wood	Percent of green weight	Percent of dry weight	Percent more heat from air-drying
Ash	45	20	21
Aspen	100	20	25
Beech, American	60	20	26
Birch, yellow	73	20	23
Douglas fir, heartwood	37	20	38
Elm, American	93	20	20
Hickory, shagbark	60	20	19
Maple, red	75	20	24
Maple, sugar	68	20	16
Oak, red	65	20	19
Oak, white	68	20	18
Pine, eastern white	68	20	10
Pine, southern yellow	70 (est.)	20	44

All the steps it takes to get ready for burning wood forces you to think in longer time spans. Because of this, you automatically become involved in a process that opens up another dimension of living intimately with the natural world. You end up not only getting ready for your stove or fireplace. You end up plugged into the satisfaction of being more independent and self-reliant.

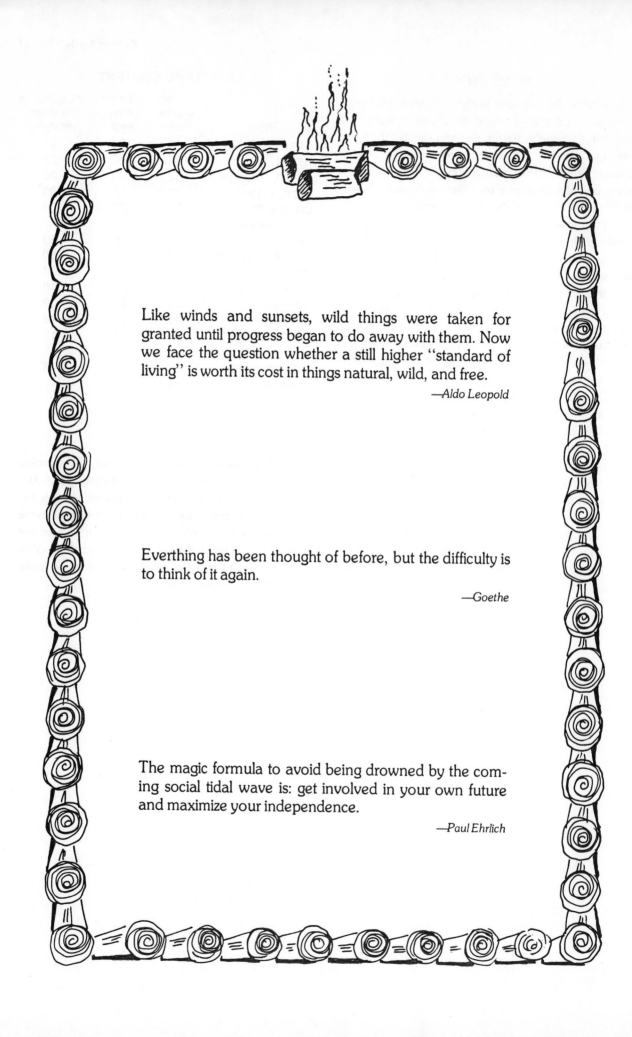

Like winds and sunsets, wild things were taken for granted until progress began to do away with them. Now we face the question whether a still higher "standard of living" is worth its cost in things natural, wild, and free.

—*Aldo Leopold*

Everthing has been thought of before, but the difficulty is to think of it again.

—*Goethe*

The magic formula to avoid being drowned by the coming social tidal wave is: get involved in your own future and maximize your independence.

—*Paul Ehrlich*

Chapter 5

AMERICAN STOVES

The variety of wood-stove designs has proliferated in the last few years, which is the good news. The bad news is that not all of them are top-notch designs. Nevertheless, it's a healthy sign that the public has a wide selection on the market to choose from, so that it is now possible to find stoves that fit nearly every room in the house, every wallet, and every sense of aesthetics.

What to look for in a stove is important, but first let's see what is generally available. (The following information is arranged alphabetically by manufacturer, not in order of preference.)

MAJOR BRANDS

Ashley

The Deluxe Imperial Model C-60 cabinet wood heater (costing about $300) can hold up to 100 pounds of 2-foot logs at a time. The mahogany enamel finish is baked on a steel cabinet with gold trim and steel meshing to give the design an ordinary furniture look. Its thermostatically controlled down-draft system is patented and works by drawing air through a small shaft where a heat-sensitive lever adjusts the air-intake opening according to the temperature. If the temperature dial is set high, the shaft opens to draw in more air to increase the fire. If the temperature dial is set low, the shaft closes to reduce air intake to retard the fire. The firebox and ash doors are airtight. Combustion air enters at the front of the firebox and flows across the logs to the flue. This results in burning the entire length of the individual logs at once. Logs are placed inside through a side door. Secondary air intake above the firebox burns wood gases for added efficiency. The C-60 model stands 3 feet high, nearly 3 feet wide, and 21 inches deep. Its shipping weight is 267 pounds. It's said to heat 4 or 5 average household rooms.

The Compact Console C-62 (costing about $280) is a smaller model of the above. It holds 50 pounds of wood up to 18 inches long. This one measures 35 inches in height, 28 inches in width, 20 inches in depth and has a shipping weight of 223 pounds. It can handle the heat for 3 or 4 rooms. With both these models the thermostat, although it isn't as highly sensitive as the usual oil-furnace thermostat, does control the burning rate of the fire and can keep a load of logs going up to 12 hours. Also available is an optional air blower that pulls heated air down through the cabinet and forces it out at floor level at 150 cubic feet per minute.

The Columbian Model 25-HF (at approximately $170) resembles the traditional wood stove. Its blue steel body encloses a separate airtight firebox. It includes a thermostat down-draft system as in the more expensive cabinet models. Logs approximately 20 inches long can be burned. The stove is set on cast-iron legs. The firebox door and top of the stove are also cast-iron. Overall measurements are 34 inches high, 20 inches wide, 30 inches deep. Shipping weight is 130 pounds.

All Ashley models have one-year warranty guarantees.

Better 'n Ben's

This wood stove is designed for existing fireplaces. A steel panel is fitted over the fireplace opening to seal off the chimney air and heat escape. Then a box stove on legs (13 inches from the panel) is adjusted to the panel. A heat deflector is tilted at a 45-degree angle above the panel to protect the mantle.

By designing for an existing fireplace, no new flue holes need to be cut into the walls or ceiling. Two inches of sand or ashes must be layered on the bottom of the firebox before the stove is lighted the first time. The heat inside the stove radiates from the 11-gauge low-carbon steel box that sits in front of the fireplace. A spark mat is placed in front of the stove box to protect the flooring or rug when the front door is opened to place more logs inside the firebox.

Altogether the stove projects 24 inches into the room. It burns 18-inch logs and will hold a fire overnight if seasoned hardwood is used. The top of the stove can be used for cooking; it measures 18 inches wide by 24 inches long.

An optional screen door is available that lets you see the fire burning. Ashes need to be removed with shovel and pail every two weeks or so. The unit fits into most of the popular-size fireplaces, but other sizes up to 60 inches wide, 48 inches high can be specially ordered. The stoves are said to heat house areas of 10,000 cubic feet or more.

The stove has a one-year warranty. Its shipping weight is 150 pounds. Prices range from $250 to $270. The free-standing stove sells for $139.

Birmingham Stove & Range Co.

The Majik Automatic is an oblong blued steel heater that takes logs up to approximately 21 inches long. It has a thermostat for heat control, stands 37 inches high, and weighs 135 pounds. The Model 32 box heater takes 30-inch logs and weighs 125 pounds.

Other wood/coal combination heaters are available in varying shapes and sizes, including the No. 21 Baron that has a steel drum for burning wood and is mounted on top of a cast-iron potbelly stove. The diameter of the firebox in the latter model is 17 inches and with the drum attached stands 63 inches high.

The 224 Knight is a cabinet wood furnace. It is constructed of cast-iron liners and is thermostatically controlled. Logs up to 24 inches can be burned. The entire unit measures 37 inches high, 35 inches wide, 21 inches deep, and weighs 306 pounds. An optional blower that is mounted under the heater at floor level to circulate warm air faster than natural convection is available.

Chimney Heat-Reclaimer Corp

The Woodmiser model has a built-in fan to circulate heat from the firebox. The fire heats a system of pipes inside the stove. Then a fan blows air through the pipes and picks up the heat, which is blown out the stove and into the rooms.

The Woodmiser stands 31 inches high, 18 inches wide, and, including the blower attachment, 27 inches deep. The firebox can handle logs up to 16 inches long. The door is double vented to supply oxygen to the wood as it burns as well as oxygen to unburned gases.

The stove is made of 24-gauge steel and has a 4-inch flue. The electricity to run the blower is figured at approximately three cents a day, the equivalent to an 80-watt light bulb. The price: $268.50.

Edison Stove Works

Two potbelly models are designed after the old-time stoves usually associated with one-room schoolhouses. They are made of cast iron and shipped disassembled. They stand 32 inches and 26 inches high. Both rest on approximately 9-inch legs.

The inside diameter of the fire pot on both models is about 9 inches and can accommodate 16-

inch logs in the larger model, 11-inch sticks in the smaller.

The stoves can be fitted to existing flue systems. Like all cast-iron stoves, the first few fires must be relatively small in order to season the iron. It's possible to crack the iron stoves if they're first subjected to intense high heat. Since the legs are made of cast iron also, the stoves must stand on noncombustible material such as stone or masonry. Also, they should be placed at least two feet from any combustible surface.

The larger potbelly stove sells for $80; the smaller, $60.

Fire-View

This modified barrel design has a glass window to see the fire as well as a steel door to contain the heat for later. Five models are available. The largest, the 360 model, has a firebox made of 12-gauge steel. Logs are placed inside by the door on the right, although left side doors can be ordered

also. Logs on the 360 model can be up to 30 inches long.

The inside diameter of the largest model is 22 inches, inside length 36 inches, and height 26 inches from fireplace hearth to top of firebox. Its firebox size has 7.91 cubic feet. All models are designed to sit in front of fireplaces that should be closed off.

The stove should rest on noncombustible stone, brick, concrete, tile, or asbestos. An optional air circulator is available that blows hot air farther and faster into the room area. It delivers 265 cubic feet of air per minute.

The glass window is tempered fireglass designed to withstand temperatures up to 550 degrees F. The 12-by-24-inch glass can be removed through a side frame for cleaning. Then a collapsible steel door behind the glass can close off the firebox to retain maximum heat value, since glass loses heat readily. The firebox is lined with firebrick. No grates are used, since circulating air passing under grates burns the fire faster. The fire is built on ashes.

An 8-inch pot holder on top of the stove can be used for cooking. Flue size for the 360 model is 7 inches (3 inches for the smallest model). With the firebrick the largest model weighs 279 pounds; without the brick, 186 pounds. Price for the largest: $388. For the smallest: approximately $200.

Fisher

Three sizes of the same stout, heavy-duty design are available—the Papa Bear, Mama Bear, Baby Bear. The stoves have two flat areas that can

be used for cooking or heating water. Steel $^1/_{14}$ of an inch or $^5/_{16}$ of an inch thick is used and more than 27 feet of welding are applied to the seams. No bolts, nuts, or asbestos is used in the construction.

Right- or left-hand door models can be ordered. All models have firebrick lining. The largest model is 32 inches long, 18 inches wide, 28 inches high, and weighs 410 pounds. A good bed of coals from seasoned hardwood can be kept live overnight or up to 12 hours. Logs up to 30 inches can be burned. On the two smaller models logs 24 inches and 18 inches can be burned.

The stoves can be returned within 90 days of installation with full refund. In addition, a 25-year guarantee on material and workmanship is granted.

Fuego III

Called a convector firebox, this unit is available in three sizes that fit fireplaces from 30 inches to 48 inches wide and 27 inches high and above. The unit encloses the fire in order to better control the air supply and burning rate. The steel firebox has tempered glass doors that can be removed for cleaning. The grate lies flat on the firebox floor. Grillework and frame are cut to fit individual fireplaces. The unit draws cool room air through vents at floor level, circulates the air up and around the heated firebox, and directs the heated air back into the room. Fires are started with both the damper and two air vents open. Once the fire is burning, the air vents and damper are gradually closed. The damper is still open 6 percent even when "closed" so that smoke escapes up the chimney. Steel doors are also available.

King

An entire line of cooking and heating stoves are available, including potbellies, wood-coal burners, and full-size kitchen ranges. One heater is the 6600 Automatic that operates by a thermostat to regulate the burning rate. It is constructed of cast-iron top and bottom, has a hinged top for loading as well as a large feed door on the front, and is said to hold a fire up to 14 hours. The firebox can take 24-inch logs. The oblong stove stands 44 inches high and has a shipping weight of 114 pounds.

Model 7801-B is an automatic wood circulator built in a cabinet style. It stands 32 inches high, 33

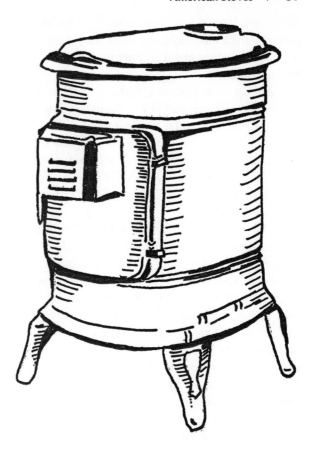

inches long, and 31 inches deep. It can take 25-inch logs. Its exterior is porcelain enamel, its interior lining of refractory firebrick. The inner unit is 18-gauge welded steel. The loading and ash-box doors are asbestos-lined to seal against air leakage. The loading door is on the right side. The cabinet top can be removed for emergency cooking surface. Its shipping weight is 215 pounds.

Locke Stove Company

The Warm-Ever stoves are barrel wood heaters that come in two sizes. Both have cast-iron doors and cast-iron legs. Model W-15 takes logs up to 15 inches in length. It is lined with 8 sections of firebrick to protect the bottom half of the barrel, which stands on its side, from burning out. Its outside dimensions are 21 inches in length, 30 inches in height, 23 inches in width, and weighs approximately 106 pounds.

Model W-24 burns firewood up to 24 inches long and is lined on the bottom with 12 sections of firebrick. Its exterior dimensions are 31 inches long,

30 inches high, 23 inches wide, and weighs 142 pounds. Both models have a draft slide door on the front loading door and a secondary draft opening at the flue outlet.

An optional warming rack, 10 inches by 14 inches, of chrome nickel is available. This is attached to the flue collar to make a flat surface over the round barrel surface in order to place kettles, pots, skillets, and other kitchen tools for warming.

A make-your-own-stove kit is also available. It includes cast-iron door, legs, and flue collar. You supply the barrel.

The wood-burning circulator Model 701 is a cabinet-style heater. It is designed with a dark-brown porcelain enamel finish, automatic draft regulator, firebrick lining, and cast-iron grates in the firebox. Includes a hinged smoke curtain to help prevent smoke from escaping when loading more fuel wood. A hinged shield on the ash box, which collects ashes by gravity below the grate, drops down when the door is opened to help keep ashes from spilling out. Firebrick lining is 2 inches thick and the cast-iron door is sealed with asbestos for tight fit. The heater stands 33 inches high, 36 inches wide, 18 inches deep, and can accept logs 26 inches in length. Shipping weight is 290 pounds. The Model 701 sells for $440. An optional blower system for it sells for $69.

Majestic

A wide range of factory-built fireplaces, free-standing fireplaces, traditional fireplaces, and gas and electric fireplaces are available. In addition, a wide range of essential equipment and accessories related to fireplaces, such as simulated brick housetop chimneys, grates, dampers, flues, and other items are available.

Fourteen different models of the Contemporary free-standing metal fireplaces are manufactured and marketed. Many of these wood-burning units are porcelain-finished in a variety of colors or matte-black finish. The Firehood model, billed as the original conical wood-burning fireplace, comes in five different porcelain colors or matte black. Two hearth sizes of 38 inches and 45 inches are made and come with fire screen, refractory hearth base, and enough pipe for an 8-foot ceiling.

The Thulman factory-built fireplaces are complete steel units and are produced with a wide range of designs and material for the surrounding facing. The metal chimney that leads from the metal firebox is a three-wall design. Cool air enters the outside cooling duct of the flue and is circulated down and around the firebox and up through the middle chamber of the chimney. This "thermo-siphoning" system allows using the cooler air as insulation while hot air is expelled at the chimney top along with smoke and wood gases. The firebox floor and walls have ceramic lining.

The Thulman fireplaces come in three sizes based on the fireplace opening—28 inches, 36 inches, 42 inches. Only the last two come in either left or right ends open for corner, room divider, or island installation. It's possible to stack the fireplaces with the individual three-wall metal flues one above the other on three different floors and still use the same brick chimney outlet.

The Old Stove Co.

Five heating stove models are available in addition to four cooking models. The Boxwood #28 model is typical. It is constructed of heavy cast iron with a firebox that can accommodate logs up to 27 inches. Dimensions are height 25 inches, length 34 inches, width 14 inches, weight 160 pounds. It uses a 6-inch stovepipe and has two cooking lids, each 8 inches in diameter. This one costs $155.

The Pot Belly #60 burns either wood or coal. It weighs 80 pounds, is 31 inches high, and has firebox dimensions of 11 inches in diameter, 15 inches in

height. This also uses a 6-inch stovepipe and has a cooking lid of 5.5 inches in diameter. The Pot Belly costs $102.

Portland Stove Foundry Co.

The Queen Atlantic model is one of the oldest cooking and warming stoves in the country. The original design was ornate and full of gadgets that fit into any old-time farmhouse kitchen. The new model No. 408 is more streamlined and less bulky but still constructed of all cast iron. The modern Queen Atlantic is adaptable to coal, oil, or wood. This six-holer has a deep ash box that does not need emptying for long periods and a brass coil for hot water. Warming ovens are available. Models with porcelain covering are also available. The height of the Queen Atlantic to the top of the range is 32

inches, overall width 57 inches, overall depth 31 inches. The firebox can easily take 21-inch logs.

A smaller four-holer wood-only cook stove is also made.

The Constitution models of the Franklin stove with folding doors are made of cast iron. They come in three sizes with each taking logs 15 inches, 18 inches, and 21 inches at the narrowest point on the inside grate. The #3 model, the largest, stands 32 inches from floor to top and weighs 290 pounds. This one is a longtime standby for Franklin stoves.

Portland Stove makes three Atlantic box stoves and two models of the Monitor style. The No. 38 Monitor has one of the largest fireboxes of all stoves made—38 inches long. The stove stands 20 inches high and has a large front door and lift covers that can accommodate especially large chunks of wood. Its overall length is 51 inches and it is designed for large rooms.

Riteway

The Riteway 2000 cabinet heater is controlled by a bimetal heat-sensitive thermostat. It can generate up to 50,000 BTUs per hour that can heat 4 or 5 rooms. It is constructed of steel plate weighing more than 3 pounds per square foot and incorporates the complete combustion design; that is, the wood gases are recirculated back through the fire to burn again, thereby extracting as much heat value as possible and reducing creosote buildup in the chimney flue. The stove comes without the optional cabinet, which costs $140 extra. With the cabinet the stove measures 36 inches long, 24 inches wide,

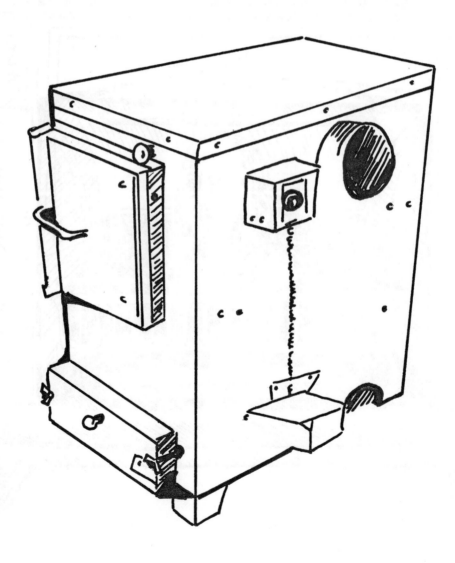

37 inches high. It can burn logs up to 24 inches long and has a wood capacity in the firebox for 4 cubic feet of fuel. The 2000 sells for $295 and weighs 225 pounds.

The LF-20 model hot-air furnace can burn wood, coal, gas, or oil and can generate 125,000 BTUs of heat per hour. With an optional burner, oil or gas automatically takes over when the wood fuel temperature falls below a certain manually set level. The LF-20 overall dimensions are 68 inches long, 34 inches wide, 53 inches high. It can accommodate 24-inch logs and has a fuel capacity of 13.5 cubic feet. It weighs 1,000 pounds and costs $1,442.

Model 37 can burn wood or coal. It is designed with a firebox that can hold up to 7½ cubic feet of fuel and can produce 73,000 BTUs per hour. The body is constructed of 14-gauge steel plate and can burn logs up to 24 inches long. The furnace stands 40 inches high, 24 inches wide, 33 inches long, and weighs 400 pounds. Without the cabinet it sells for $395; with the cabinet, $516.

Shenandoah

Model R-75 is an upright barrel-type heater. It uses a bimetal thermostat on the door to adjust the air intake. Asbestos rope around the doorjamb keeps the firebox airtight. The firebrick lining reaches 9 inches high along the sides of the 10-inch-diameter cast-iron grate. The loading door is 12 by 13 inches. The top and door are constructed of 11-gauge steel, the exterior jacket 18-gauge. The stove stands 35 inches high, 24 inches in diameter, and uses a 6-inch pipe flue. It weighs 164 pounds. With a low flame, a fire can last 12 hours.

Model R-55 is a similar upright barrel-style heater that uses both wood or coal.

Model R-76 is a black porcelain-finish cabinet wood and coal heater. It is an airtight design with bimetal thermostat control that limits the amount of secondary air supplied above the fire to burn wood gases. The model stands 24 inches wide, 35 inches long, 36 inches high, and weighs 260 pounds.

The Fire-Grate comes with either 6 or 7 tubes made of 14-gauge steel with a 2-inch diameter. The unit is placed in the fireplace and plugged into any standard 115-volt outlet. The 61-watt blower circulates 100 cubic feet of air a minute. The blower can be mounted on either side of the grate and can generate up to 50,000 BTUs. The 7-tube grate

measures 24 inches high, 20 inches deep, 31 inches wide at the front, 23 inches wide at the back. A speed control box is optional.

United States Stove Company

Two boxwood stoves made of heavy-gauge steel are named 126-S and 132-S. The larger second one can take logs up to 32 inches; the smaller, up to 26 inches long. Both use 6-inch flues and have manual adjustable draft slide openings on the door to help control the heat. The stoves weigh 95 and 110 pounds and, except for the legs, come fully assembled.

The Wonderwood is a cabinet-style automatic wood circulator. Logs are placed inside the airtight firebox by a side door. The doors are sealed with asbestos and the firebox is lined with firebrick. An optional blower is available that circulates the heated air at floor level. The Wonderwood can burn logs up to 26 inches. The stove stands 33 inches high, 19 inches wide, and 32 inches long. It uses a 6-inch flue; its shipping weight is 220 pounds. A nonelectrical thermostat regulates the temperature automatically.

The Franklin is the traditional folding-door fireplace-stove combination. It stands about 31 inches high and 43 inches deep. It can handle logs about 23 inches long. The entire stove weighs about 250 pounds. The frame is made of cast iron; the hearth, firebox, and main top are made of steel plate. Wood, coal, and charcoal can be burned in it. Optional accessories include a barbecue grille, grate basket, fire screen, brass knobs, bean pot and hook, and other additions.

Vermont Techniques, Inc.

Panels described as a fireplace stove are placed to protrude and enclose a fireplace in order to control the draft. Folding doors allow the fire to be seen when desired. With the doors closed at night and with a fire banked in ashes, the heat effect can be prolonged.

The panels are made of ⅛-inch steel plate and painted black. Two basic sizes are standard, but special fitting for unusual fireplaces can be ordered. The sizes are 31 inches high by 40 inches wide and 35 inches high by 44 inches wide. Option features include a curtain mesh screen, a system of heat pipes to increase output, and a warming shelf for food or drink. The units cost $152 and $160.

Vermont Woodstove Co.

The Down Drafter model is designed to burn wood gases by circulating them back over the coal bed. The body is airtight with continuously welded seams on the steel. The firebox is constructed of chrome nickel-steel alloy. It has a separate ash-removal door at the bottom of the loading door, which is 9 inches by 10 inches.

The firebox takes up to 24-inch logs and has a loading capacity of 5 cubic feet of wood or 1/25 of a cord. Its overall measurements are 31 inches high, 26 inches wide, 34 inches long. The blower adds another 10 inches. Its heating capability is said to be 60,000 BTUs per hour and can heat 5 or 6 rooms. It costs $489.

A smaller model takes 18-inch logs, has a heating capability of up to 20,000 BTUs per hour, and measures 25 inches by 22 inches by 28 inches. It has no blower attached. It costs $289. Both models are guaranteed against defects in material and workmanship for one year.

Washington Stove Works

The Parlor Stove has fuel loading doors on the front and the side. The difference in the five models is not the size, which is the same, but in the decorative trim. Model V, for example, has as optional additions a nickel-plated swing top and nickel-plated foot rail, top rail, and door frame to set off the all-black color of the basic unit. The stove can be ordered without the base and legs to set directly on a noncombustible hearth. The standard unit measures 31 inches high, 25 inches wide, 22 inches deep, and weighs 180 pounds. A spark guard for use when the front door is left open is available.

The Camper's Companion weighs 30 pounds and can be dismantled to pack into backcountry or to a cabin. It measures 28 inches high and 12 inches wide and can be used with any fuel.

Three box heaters are available. The Arctic and King Models are made of all cast iron while the Marco Sun is made with the top, bottom, and inside lining of cast iron and with the exterior of blued steel. The Arctic is the largest at 34 inches deep, 15 inches wide, 26 inches high. It weighs 110 pounds.

All three have a swing top for loading large fuel wood as well as front doors for smaller pieces.

Norwester Model 38 is a cabinet-style wood circulating heater. It uses a thermostat for heat output control and has cast-iron lining. The top grille swings open, but it also has a side loading door. A factory-installed assist fan is an optional feature. The exterior comes in blond or brown porcelain enamel. The stove stands 32 inches high, 29 inches wide, 21 inches deep, and can accept logs up to 24 inches long. Shipping weight is 270 pounds.

Yankee Woodstove

This drum stove comes in four models, one of them horizontal to take 24-inch logs. The barrels are custom-made of 18-gauge carbon steel. The doors are cast iron and the fastenings are steel-riveted. The horizontal Model 28 measures 29 inches long, 27 inches high from the floor, and about 18 inches wide.

The airtight design can keep a fire going up to 10 hours without reloading. An internal baffle system burns the wood gases for added efficiency.

The upright Model 18 uses 18-inch logs, the smaller Model 15 burns 15-inch logs. The upright models can be used for cooking or heating food and drink. Shipping weight for the heaviest model is 35 pounds. All models have an adjustable 3-inch-diameter draft control on the door. They cost approximately $60 and are guaranteed for 3 years.

WHAT TO LOOK FOR

No single stove fits everyone's needs or wants. This is the reason why it's impossible to say which stove is the best and should be recommended for all purposes. That's like saying a Rolls Royce is the best car on the road and should be driven by everyone. Not only is a Rolls not the best car for backcountry dirt-road messing around, but also it can't be bought by everyone. Besides, the company is out of business!

For wood stoves, however, certain features should be kept in mind as they fit into your overall plan of heating you and your home with wood. They are:

Workmanship

Look to see if the welding is done evenly without any visible sign of air bubbles or cracks. Be

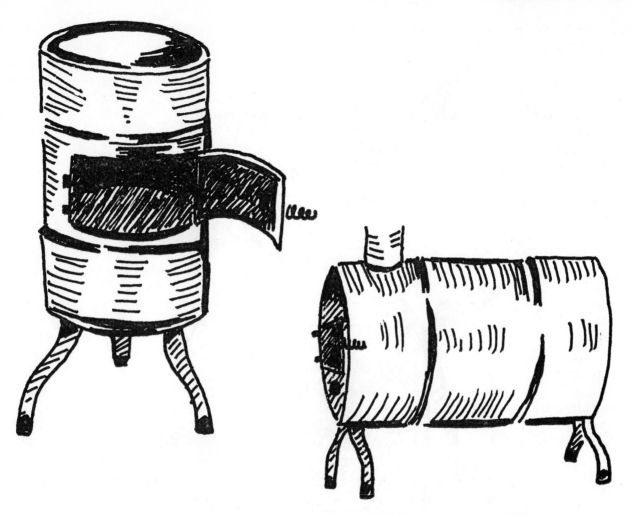

sure that the seams fit tightly, that the door closes flush against the body of the stove, and that it doesn't slip back slightly once you close it. If it does, air leaks will definitely rob you of heat efficiency.

The black paint should be evenly applied. No blotches or weak marks should be visible. The firebox lining should be fitted perfectly. Any hinges should be solid and snugly fitted. So should any cooking-pot lids. Any excessive sliding back and forth of the pot-holder lid plates can cause air leaks. Make certain that the stove rests squarely on the floor without tilting and that no wedges are slipped under the legs to even it for selling.

Take a good long look at the firebox. This is the heart of your stove. If any slight cracks are seen, they could cause trouble and grief later on. One good way to test the airtightness of a firebox, if you have the opportunity, is to set a fire going in it in a dark room. If a flicker of light comes from the stove, then the stove has a crack in it.

It's impossible to do this in a showroom, but if you're searching to buy a stove, it would be good to take a flashlight along with you to peer inside the fireboxes. Usually they're painted black and without some additional concentrated light giving the interior a good, thorough examination is next to impossible.

Cast Iron or Sheet Metal

In the old days anybody worth his salt had a cast-iron stove, mainly because that was about all they made. Today many people swear by the cast-iron stove and won't try any other. Cast iron has been improved with ferromanganese processes, but so has the steel sheet metal.

Both cast iron and steel are ferrous base metals

and therefore both will rust—the reason most of the stoves are covered with black sicon paint that withstands intense heat. Technical differences between the two materials make the choice less automatic. For example, steel has approximately three times the tensile strength of cast iron as well as approximately a 500-degree higher melting temperature.

How this applies to stoves is another matter, however. Cast iron definitely holds heat much longer after the fire dies out. Cast iron is sturdier and tends to wear better against continuous heat; it won't crack for many years, if ever.

Steel stoves, on the other hand, are lighter, more easily transported. They can be moved about in the home. Sheet metal heats up much more quickly to conduct heat faster, but it also loses its heat almost as fast as the fire dies out. Unless the fires are well controlled and not allowed to rise to overintense temperatures, sheet-metal stoves can warp and break the seal of the seams faster than cast iron. Whether this takes two years or ten years depends on how well the stove is cared for.

Sheet-metal stoves are also less expensive. Small parlor stoves, for example, can be purchased for $20 and used now and then to heat a small room. However, it's wise to examine the thickness of the metal of any size sheet-metal stove and to stay clear of any that is less than $1/16$ of an inch thick.

In general, good sheet-metal stoves that will do the job are available at inexpensive prices. So are cast-iron stoves. Simply bear in mind that because a stove is cast iron does not necessarily mean it is well-made, nor does sheet metal always imply that the stove will warp in a year. It depends on how the two metals are used.

Convenience of Use

Since wood stoves must be attended to two or three or more times a day, depending on their individual efficiencies, they should be designed for optimum convenience. Therefore, compare the stoves that appeal to you in terms of ease of use.

Make sure that the door handle isn't going to be too hot to touch, that the door itself is large enough to put logs in without squeezing and stuffing them through a relatively small hole, that the stove is high enough for you without going to your knees every time you reload.

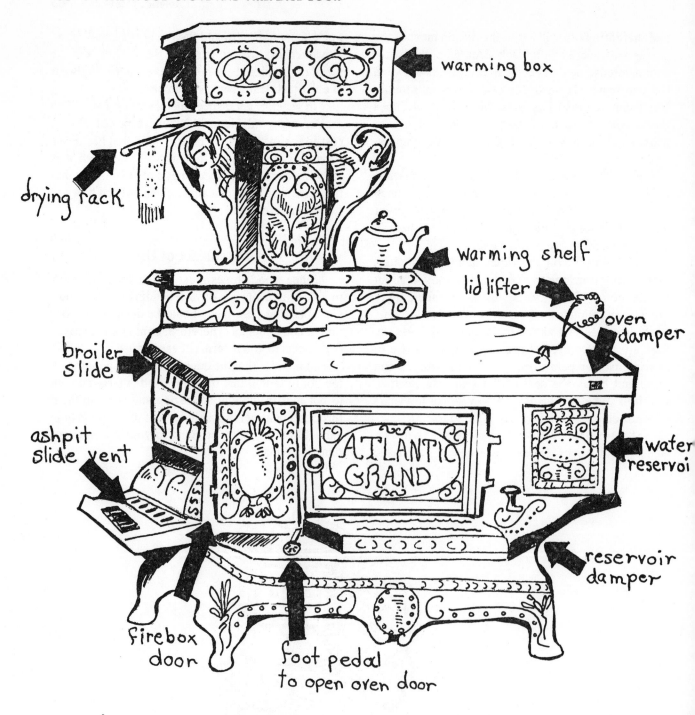

warming box

drying rack

warming shelf

lid lifter

oven damper

broiler slide

ashpit slide vent

water reservoi

reservoir damper

firebox door

foot pedal to open oven door

Anticipate how easily the ashes can be removed, how difficult the stove will be to install, whether or not you will be able to place a kettle of water on top of it, whether it will block too much of your living space. A side-door design may be more convenient than a front-door design. Then again, it may not. See whether or not it has a pot-holder lid handle and slot, whether or not full heat comes from all four sides or merely the front half, in case you may want to turn it at different angles according to your house plan.

If it doesn't have an automatic thermostat control, make certain that the manual draft control is easy to touch and use. Check the flue damper handle to see whether it is inside the stove or outside. In short, think not only in terms of efficient heat production but also of how easy or difficult it is to get the heat production in the first place.

BUYING OLD STOVES

In 1906 Sears and Roebuck advertised a grand old cast-iron wood-burning six-holder cooking stove with elaborate decoration, engraving, and shiny silver metal for $15.95. And that was new. Now that 1906 stove sells for ten or twenty times that amount, if you can find a used one.

However, if you do find an old stove, you should take a very close look at it. If an old stove has been used for a number of years—and some have been worked for decades at a time—chances are that wear and tear on it have taken some toll. The stove may indeed be in tip-top shape: many are. Nevertheless, take the time to cast an objective eye upon it.

The outside may be perfectly intact, but it is the firebox that should be examined very carefully. Look it over inch by inch if you can, especially the corners and seams. Look for cracks, the main culprits that reduce efficiency.

Small cracks can probably be repaired, but large ones will cause only havoc. If you spot the big cracks, do your best to say no to buying the old gem. It'll be difficult to say no to a big old loving ornate potbellied grandfather, but in the long run you'll save yourself both wood and personal energy.

Society is always taken by surprise at any new example of commonsense.

—*Emerson*

We calculate that each ton of recycled waste paper saves 17 trees and that the current recycling activity conserves close to 200 million trees annually. This is equal to the annual yield of 5 million acres of woodland.

—*Edwin Locke*

The blessing is not in living but in living well.

—*Seneca*

Chapter 6

SCANDINAVIAN STOVES

Only a few years ago the use of imported wood stoves in this country was minimal, but today a much larger selection of foreign stoves are on the American market. Of all the imported stoves in the United States, those from Norway and Denmark have received most acceptance.

In general, the Scandinavian stoves are designed differently from the American stoves and require a slightly different method of attention. Before taking a look at some of these foreign stoves available here, knowing two of the basic differences is helpful.

AIRTIGHTNESS

The majority of American stoves are not constructed for airtightness. On the other hand, the far greater majority of Scandinavian stoves are. As a result, different principles govern how wood is burned.

In most American stoves the logs normally burn the full length at the same time. They are usually wrapped in flames from one end to the other, since most fireboxes are not airtight enough to control the oxygen supply strictly. Either the design promotes full log burning or false drafts leak into the firebox to create full burning.

In the Scandinavian stoves the firebox is completely sealed so that the air supply can be highly regulated by small sealable holes usually in the doors. Because of this, oxygen enters only at the front of the stove and is used at that point only to burn the wood. In turn, the logs, placed straight in lengthwise, burn where the oxygen first comes in contact with the fire and wood, that is, the logs burn from end to end like a candle.

Most Scandinavian stoves also include a sec-

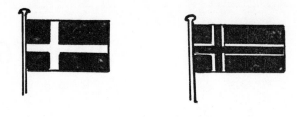

ondary air-intake aperture. Oxygen from this source is used to burn the wood gases after the first burning. That way as much of the wood-fuel potential as possible is burned. The secondary air-intake valve is usually located above the primary valve so that the secondary supply moves directly to where the wood gases pass on their way to the chimney flue.

Although certainly not exclusive to Scandinavian stoves (some American stoves have this feature), it is this airtightness principle that in general adds extra measures of efficiency to heating with wood. By controlling the air supply the heat intensity of the fire can be controlled. With experience comes the expertise of drawing as much heat as you can from the wood without wasting it.

BAFFLES

The second conspicuous feature of Scandinavian stoves is the baffle system. Nearly all of them have internal baffles or iron plates that force the wood gases and heat to travel farther inside the stove before escaping into the chimney. By forcing the heat to remain inside the stove as long as possi-

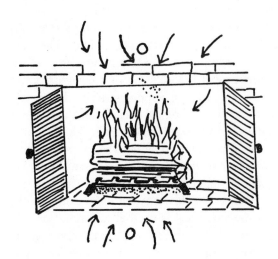

ble, more of the heat is absorbed by the cast iron to be radiated into the living area.

In some models the baffles force the heat to travel in an *S* pattern. In other models baffles and passageways keep the heat in the stove available to the house twice as long as would a stove that has no baffle, which allows the gases to travel directly from the burning logs into the chimney.

Most baffle systems can be seen by merely peering into the firebox. Not all models have them, so take a look. They can save you fuel.

MAJOR BRANDS

Fyrtonden

Four models made in Denmark range in price from $540 to $715. Each is barrel-shaped and constructed from 4 mm plate steel. Model A, the largest, stands 34 inches high with a diameter of 23 inches. All models come with option of top or rear smoke outlets. Models C and D are available, at $36 extra, with ring stove lids for cooking. The front is open, so one can view the fire set on grates. The secondary air-intake valve is located above the opening.

Jotul

Model 118 is Jotul's standard wood heater. Built of all cast iron, its airtight firebox can generate heat up to 12 hours on the end-to-end burning principle. It burns logs up to 24 inches long and is said to have a heating capacity for 7,000 cubic feet of room space. The stove measures 30 inches high, 14 inches wide, 29 inches long, and has a shipping weight of 231 pounds.

As with other models, this one comes with either dark-green or subdued-red enamel. Most

Scandinavians wonder why Americans want to have the black-paint models that need blacking now and then to keep them looking respectable. Enamel over all parts of the exterior eliminates the need for blacking and keeps the general appearance the same throughout the use of the stove.

Enamel on the Jotul is melted glass that is baked in two layers. It can withstand temperature of about 1,100 degrees Fahrenheit. Enamel can develop hairline cracks, bubbles, and eventual peeling if continued high heat is inflicted upon it, but with the draft control this seldom occurs. If the enamel does crack, repair materials are available.

Factory tests in Norway resulted in a 76 percent fuel use efficiency when 3.1 pounds of seasoned wood with 20 percent moisture content was burned per hour. That meant 24 percent of the heat potential went up the stack. By comparison, other sources indicate that standard open fireplaces are about 10 percent efficient and Franklin stoves 25 percent. The same Jotul 118 model resulted in 54.8 percent efficiency to generate 44,500 BTUs when burning 11 pounds of wood per hour.

The baffle compartment is a chamber above the main firebox. Logs are placed straight in on a bed of sand and coals. The logs burn at the point closest to the draft controls on the door. As the logs burn toward the rear of the firebox, the resulting heat and wood gases take longer to escape through the flue at the rear of the upper chamber. When the logs have burned down to all coals, the coals are raked to the front. Then new logs are placed on top of the coals that ignites them. The process begins again.

The 118 sells for approximately $400, $45 extra for the enameled models. The 602 model is a smaller version of the 118. Jotul has other wood stoves for

cooking as well as fireplace stoves and combination heater-fireplace designs.

Kalorius

This fireplace-stove combination is designed with a donut-shaped top to keep the hot wood gases inside the stove and house as long as possible. Hinged doors convert it to a fireplace or heater. Constructed of plate steel and of Danish design, the open port can be used as a warming grate. Barbecue grille, floor plate, and wall rack for tool storage are all available for an extra $150. The stove stands 59 inches to the top of the flue, 20 inches wide, 15 inches deep. Stove alone costs $850.

Lange

All stoves from this Danish manufacturer are made from cast iron. The doors are hand-filed to fit tightly and all joints are sealed with cement. Nearly all models have two draft regulators for primary and secondary air intakes and nearly all have baffle systems.

The 6303 model is an arch design that can be used for a warming plate. The internal baffle is located at the top of the arch in order to extract up to 20 percent more heat from the firebox. The stove stands 37 inches high, 16 inches wide, 25 inches long. It can burn 18-inch logs and can heat an area up to 6,000 cubic feet. It weighs 220 pounds to ship and costs $415 for the porcelain model, $325 for the black iron finish.

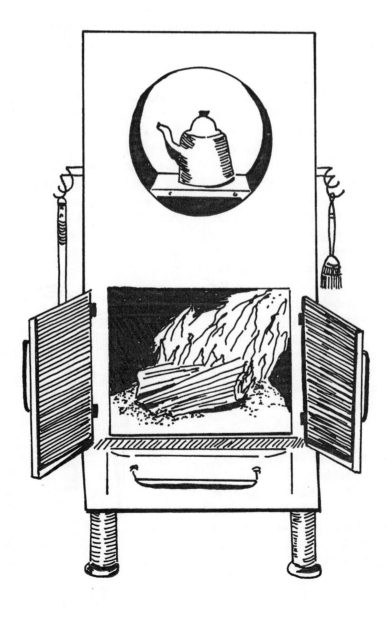

The 6302A model is 34 inches high, 15 inches wide, 34 inches long, and can burn logs up to 24 inches long. It weighs 272 pounds and is said to generate enough heat to warm up to 9,000 cubic feet. This one sells for $495 for the porcelain finish, $425 for the black iron.

Lange also puts out a fireplace-stove combination, the 61MF model. This high, narrow design takes a teepee fire of 16-inch logs. It stands 38 inches high, 20 inches wide, 19 inches deep, and is said to be as effective as a regular heater stove. Its capacity is said to be up to 7,000 cubic feet. Small panes of glass in the doors let you see the fire burning. The doors can be opened while the fire is burning or completely replaced with a spark screen. With the doors closed, it acts as a heater. The firebox interior is lined with firebrick.

Morso

This fireplace-stove combination, Morso 1125, from Denmark is cast iron that comes in matte-black or gloss-olive-green porcelain finish. Its clean, contemporary design stands 42 inches high, 29 inches wide, 23 inches deep. Logs 18 inches long can be burned and the fire can be seen through a screen attached to the opening. The screen is stored on a hook under the stove. The hinged doors are lined with gaskets so that they can be closed tightly for overnight heat. Up to 5,000 cubic feet of space can be heated. Cost, $495.

Model 6B is another contemporary design taken after the traditional box-stove shape. Its loading door is on top of the stove. This door is gasketed to prevent air leaks and false drafts. It stands 24 inches high, 14 inches wide, 23 inches long, and burns logs up to 16 inches long. Its shipping weight is 110 pounds and it is said to heat up to 2,000 cubic feet. It costs $295.

Styria

This Austrian wood stove, the one exception to our Scandinavian chapter title, is noticeable for its narrow depth. It comes in three models, the largest of which is 18 inches deep. (The other two are both 15 inches deep.) Model 4 also has a total height of 48

inches and a width of 22 inches. All three models have fireboxes that are lined on all four sides and the bottom with firebrick and can burn logs 12 inches long. Both the fuel door and ash-box door have key-lock knobs. The largest model weighs 533 pounds and comes with nickel-plated trim and fittings on an overall green enamel facing. It sells for $1,220. Model 4 in all black steel and black iron sells for $900.

Trolla

The 102 model from Norway is one of the smallest stoves made. It stands 24 inches high, 11 inches wide, 17 inches long and burns logs 12 inches long. Its heating capacity is said to cover up to 3,200 cubic feet. The stove costs $229 and has a shipping weight of 76 pounds.

Trolla makes the 105 model that burns 16-inch logs and the 107 model that burns 24-inch logs. They are basically the same but larger box-stove heaters as the 102.

The 800 model is a fireplace-stove combination. It is designed in a modified pyramid shape with overall dimensions of 41 inches high, 25 inches wide, 20 inches deep. It weighs 300 pounds and uses a heavy-duty grate as a fire bed. Logs are burned in an upright teepee style. A fire screen allows the flames to be seen while the cast-iron door can be tightly shut for maximum heat retention.

WHAT TO LOOK FOR

Most Scandinavian stoves show fine craftsmanship in the tooling and the design, but that is no reason alone to accept a particular stove without examining it carefully and individually. Lemons do get out of the factory, so take a close look at the cemented seams for any cracks. Make sure that the doors have gaskets to block all air leaks. If doors do not have designs for gaskets, look to see that they close tightly. One good test is to place a piece of paper at the doorjamb, close the door and lock it, and then tug at the paper. The hand-tooled models should fit snugly and not release the paper. If the paper comes out easily, then the door is not faced evenly and air will escape.

Always look for the baffle system, if you want

one in your stove, because not all models incorporate them, especially the fireplace-stove combinations. Also, shop around for the best price. The imported stoves are rising in price because the demand is rising. The best time to buy them is in late winter and spring and summer when the fall and early winter rush is over and dealers have leftovers. Usually, sale prices appear on the same model stoves.

Keep a critical eye on the stated heating capacity. How many cubic feet a particular stove heats is an extremely shaky estimate. The variables range from not only how well your house is insulated to how well you maintain the fire but also the inflated figures of wishful advertising. Remember that no independent research laboratory has ever conducted a test of the efficiency of a wide range of both American and Scandinavian stoves.

In buying a stove, make careful, thoughtful judgments on the size you realistically need. If you don't get the right size stove for a particular room or house, you may end up with unnecessary troubles. Too small a stove can urge you to overheat it so that you waste wood and possibly damage the stove. Too large a stove may force you to keep the fire down low so that too much creosote is released to clog up your flue. The tolerances for too small and too large a stove are wide, but they are not infinite. An accurate assessment of your needs, however, will eliminate problems before they have a chance to get started. From then on, it's a hot time in the old house tonight!

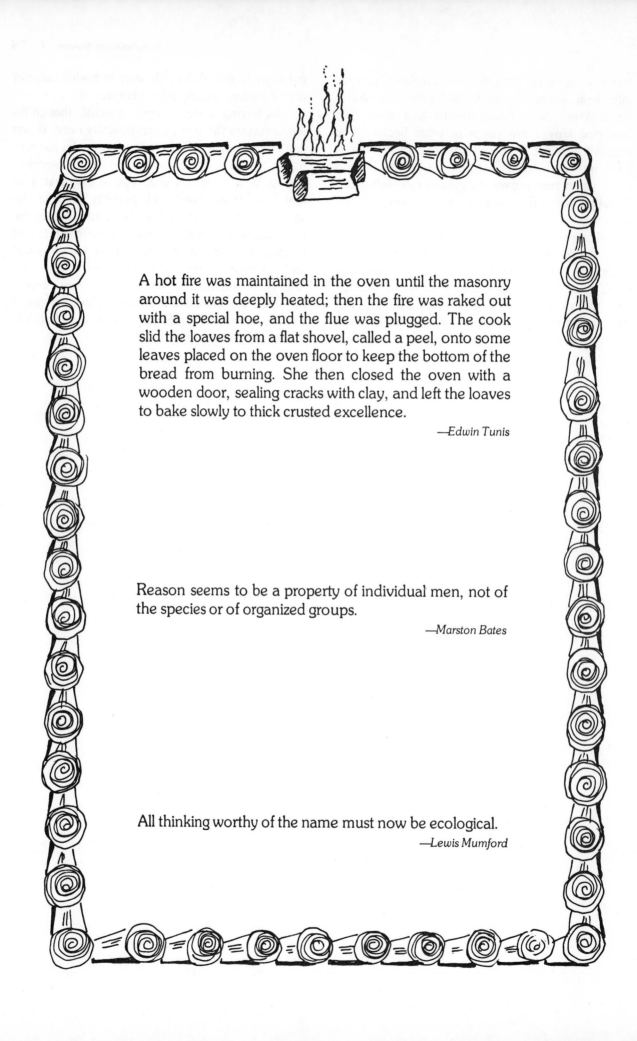

A hot fire was maintained in the oven until the masonry around it was deeply heated; then the fire was raked out with a special hoe, and the flue was plugged. The cook slid the loaves from a flat shovel, called a peel, onto some leaves placed on the oven floor to keep the bottom of the bread from burning. She then closed the oven with a wooden door, sealing cracks with clay, and left the loaves to bake slowly to thick crusted excellence.

—Edwin Tunis

Reason seems to be a property of individual men, not of the species or of organized groups.

—Marston Bates

All thinking worthy of the name must now be ecological.

—Lewis Mumford

Chapter 7

FIREPLACES AND DO-IT-YOURSELF STOVES

Heating directly by fire no doubt began millennia ago when primitive families in makeshift shelters burned branches and animal dung in a ring of rocks—the first fireplaces. When shelters became more permanent, so did the heating and cooking system. Rocks on the floor became bricks in a chimney.

Today fireplaces are built into many, if not most, houses. Through the years their design has been everything from gigantic walk-in pig-roasting fire rooms to petite showcases that don't make a decent dent on life whatsoever. Brick fireplaces are still the standard fare, but the free-standing steel fireplaces are probably the most commercially widespread innovation in recent years.

Whatever the style, the most workable principles of fireplaces are nearly 200 years old and people who abide by them swear by them.

COUNT RUMFORD

Benjamin Thompson (1753–1814) (titled as Count Rumford) was the man who first laid down the theory of fireplaces. He was one of the many extraordinary experimenters of the eighteenth and nineteenth centuries. Born in Woburn, Massachusetts, he remained loyal to King George III and left with the British for London when Boston was abandoned to the rebel Revolutionaries of the new America in 1776. He made his way to Austria and by focusing his ambition on the right political moves he rose from one important position to the next. Finally, in 1791 he was made a count of the Holy Roman Empire. He took as his title the name of his wife's family township, which at that time was Rumford. Today it is Concord, New Hampshire.

Rumford had always been fascinated by chemical and mechanical forces and studied them in

one form or another wherever he traveled. In London he concentrated on improving the bothersome smoky chimneys that everyone in those days relied upon for space heating and cooking. In the tradition of the era, he set himself a practical problem he wished to solve and by doing so developed general theories that are applicable today.

One of his basic discoveries was that the heat from fireplaces heats primarily by radiation, not by conduction or convection. In other words, straight-arrow rays from the fire burst out and heat solid objects such as floors, walls, furniture, and people. The intervening air is not heated (one reason that direct-fire heat feels dry and comfortable). Air immediately surrounding these heated objects or the fireplace itself is, however, warmed by the rays heating the solid objects, that is, by conduction.

To follow through with his discovery, Rumford constructed fireplaces according to strict basic calculations. In London he and his assistants reconstructed 500 fireplaces based on his principles.

The name of Count Rumford became associated with fireplaces that did not smoke and that radiated additional heat into the rooms.

His fundamental principles were that, first, the middle of the throat of the chimney must line up with the middle point of the floor of the fireplace. Secondly, a shelf must be built into the chimney above the hearth so that hot air rises up one side of the flue and cold air from the outside falls partway down the other half of the chimney. This provides a continuous revolution of air and creates a strong draft that sends the smoke—and flames—shooting up the chimney instead of into the house. We now call this a smoke shelf. It's an utterly simple design, but at the time it was revolutionary because chimneys before Count Rumford were almost no chimneys at all.

Rumford specifies that the chimney throat (where we now locate a movable metal plate damper to regulate the size of the opening) must be four inches wide. The specification must be followed whether the fireplace is three feet across or eight. He also specifies that the slope of the fire-back wall be angled forward to radiate the heat rays in straight lines into the rooms at multiple angles.

Fireplaces must not be as deep as most are constructed today, but shallow and high. Such a design projects more heat rays efficiently. Rumford's calculation is that the width of the back wall must be the same distance as the back wall is to the front of the fireplace. With the side walls of the fireplace slanted, these shallow dimensions will increase heat projection while, in conjunction with the narrow draft-creating throat, keep smoke rising totally up the flue, where it belongs.

FRANKLIN FIREPLACE

Even with Count Rumford's advances in constructing fireplaces, to this day scarcely more than 10 pounds of wood heat value goes into the room for every 100 pounds burned. Fireplaces are approximately 10 percent efficient, or in more heartrending terms, 90 percent of their potential goes up the chimney.

Ben Franklin also knew how inefficient fire-places were (he figured 17 percent efficiency) and did something about it around the same time as Count Rumford was working on his improvements. Franklin is sometimes credited with being the first to box a fireplace. The Pennsylvania Five Plate, as the stove was called, could be attached to a wall. The stove would stand in the bedroom and coals would be shoveled from the kitchen fire through the wall directly into the stove.

The advantage of the metal being capable of radiating more heat than a brick fireplace (which Rumford recommended) appealed to Franklin's practicality, but his aesthetic sense was not satisfied. He himself enjoyed seeing a fire flickering away and he knew others did, too. So, being the great compromiser he was, he designed the 1742 Pennsylvania Stove by increasing the heat output of a fireplace without eliminating the essence of a fireplace in the process.

What he did was to enclose the front of the fireplace by sloping glass or metal doors. He arranged for the oxygen supply for the fire to be tunneled

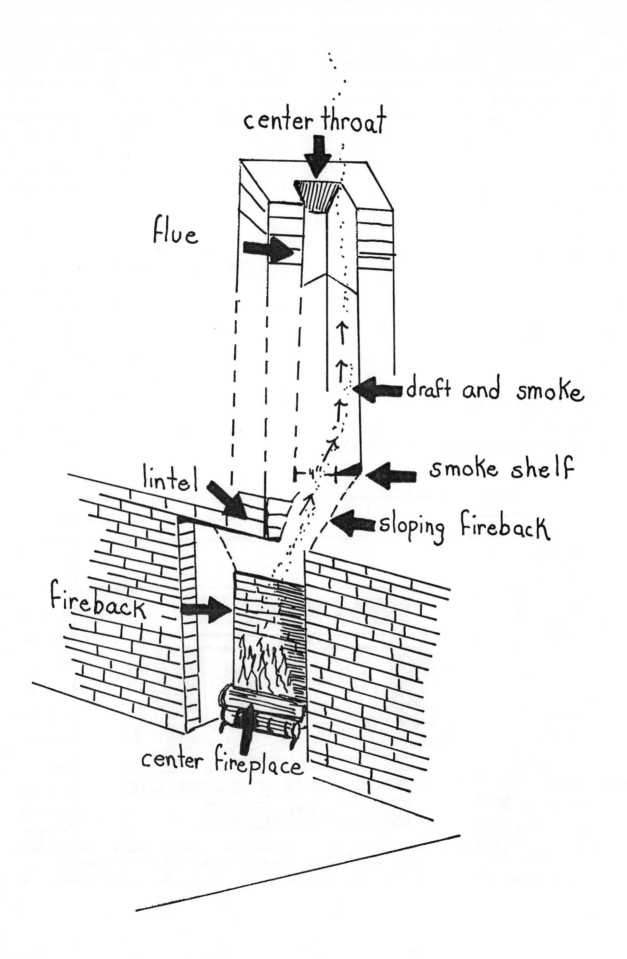

center throat

flue

draft and smoke

smoke shelf

lintel

sloping fireback

fireback

center fireplace

from outside the house rather than exhausting it from the room and therefore having to open windows. Then he built a barrier behind the hearth but in front of the chimney and attached his door contraption. This sealed off false drafts from both the chimney and the living area. If metal, the door could be opened so that one might see the flames, closed to increase heat output. It was simple, ingenious, and the forerunner of contemporary designs.

What we now call Franklin stoves stem from the Pennsylvania Five Plate, not Franklin's fireplace design. Modifications of Franklin's fireplace idea, however, are currently on the market.

FIREPLACES

Included here are both fireplaces as such and fireplace additions that are designed to increase heat output.

American Stovalator

This unit fits directly into the fireplace to enclose the fire and decrease the amount of heated air lost up the chimney. It is constructed of steel plate and has tempered glass doors and poured refractory cement on the fire-chamber floor. No grate is used. The fire is built directly on the cement. Cool room air is drawn through portholes under the unit and heated by the fire as the air circles the unit to come out the holes at the top of the unit. Wood gases and fumes escape up the chimney. The enclosed fire is said to save up to 40 percent of fuel wood. The standard unit that completely fronts the fireplace costs $349.

Birmingham Stove & Range Co.

Two basic free-standing steel fireplaces are available, both similar. Model 139 has its hearth cut at a wide slanting backward angle to more than 38 inches to give a wider view of the fire. It is 28 inches deep and 41 inches high to the start of the 8-inch-diameter flue. It comes in matte-black and burnt-orange porcelain enamel and has a shipping weight of 165 pounds. A fire screen is included, but the grate is optional. The fireplace can also be used for gas or electric logs.

Circ-U-lator

This fireplace grate is a system of hollow square pipes connected to an enclosed air fan. It measures 20 inches by 21 inches by 21 inches and is substituted for the simple traditional iron grate. A fire is built directly on this unit and heats the air in the pipes, while the fan circulates the heated air through the pipes and out into the room. Smoke and gases from the fire rise as usual directly up the chimney. The blower rests to the side of the hearth. Model 660 circulates 60 cubic feet of air a minute; model 6100, 100 cubic feet a minute. The blower consumes 60 watts an hour. Cost, $140.

Eagle Hearth Heater

This hollow-tube grate system on Model 24 has 15 tubes made of 16-gauge steel. The fan circulates 252 cubic feet of air per minute. The fire is built directly on the grate. The blower unit stretches across the front of the fireplace as it draws room air in, blows it through the heated hollow pipes, and returns it to the room. Smoke rises as usual up the chimney. The blower unit is 51 inches long, the grate 30 inches wide into the fireplace. The basic standard unit is $200; the deluxe unit with spark screen and fan enclosure is $319.

Heat-catcher

Style B is a series of 9 tubes that encircle the fire in a fireplace. A blower draws in 150 cubic feet of air a minute and channels it through the tubes being heated by the fire and out again through a vent at floor level. The tubes have 1,269 square inches of surface, the entire unit 3,000 square inches. Five sizes are available. The largest, 48B, stands 25 inches high, has a back width of 32 inches, a front width of 38 inches, and is 14 inches deep. It uses $1\frac{1}{2}$-inch-diameter, 16-gauge steel. It costs $369.

Style E has 8 heating tubes. A solid steel plate is used as the grate on the bottom and is said to

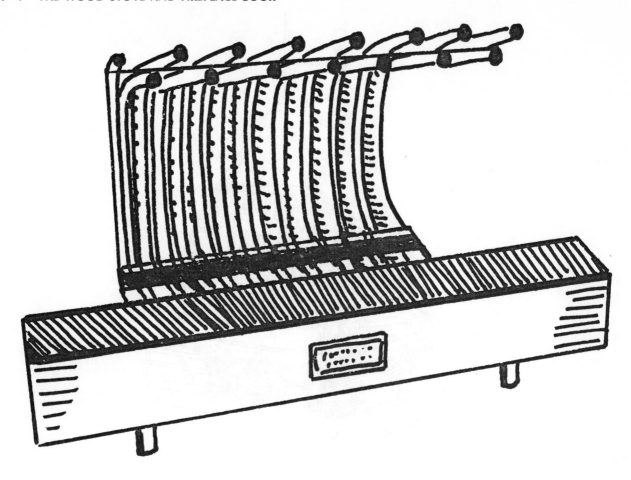

prevent burnout of the tubes. This model stands 25 inches high, has a back width of 21 inches, a front width of 23 inches, and a depth of 19 inches. It also uses $1^1/_2$-diameter tubes of 16-gauge steel. It costs $200.

Style S is not recommended for the average home. It has 18 heating tubes, a blower, and a standard design grate. It stands 28 inches high, 33 inches wide in the back, 35 inches wide at the front, and is 21 inches deep. It sells for $587.

Heatilator

The Mark C is a complete internal fireplace unit designed to circulate more heat back into the living area. The steel firebox includes metal throat, damper, and down-draft shelf, and the smoke dome that a standard masonry fireplace does. Masonry is added around the unit. Cold air ducts draw in fresh air from the floor level; warm air ducts channel heated air back into the room above the mantle. Five models have finished widths up to 60 inches,

finished height up to 36 inches, once the masonry or other fireplace facing is completed. A twenty-year guarantee comes with it.

Lance

This hollow grate-fan system measures 22 inches high, 21 inches wide, 18 inches deep and weighs 34 pounds. The five curved tubes are $1^1/_2$ inches in diameter and 24 inches in length. The fire is built directly on the tubes, while the blower draws in cool room air at floor level and forces the heated air out the top. The fan unit sits near the hearth. Cost, $91.

Malm

Thirteen different models of free-standing fireplaces are available. All are made of steel and colored with porcelain enamel fired at 1,400 degrees. The height of the burning unit, excluding the flue, ranges from 29 inches to 90 inches, de-

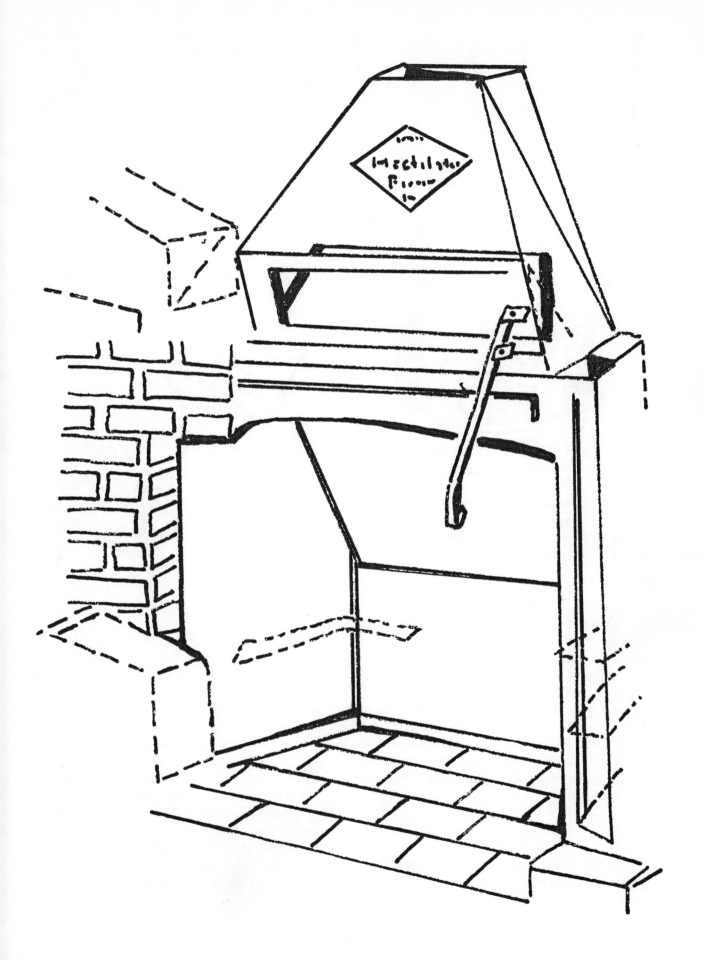

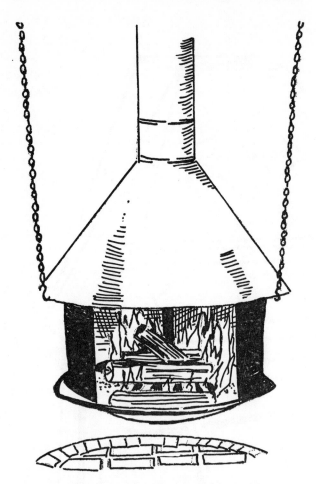

pending on the design. The Fire Duchess model is suspended on steel chains from the ceiling and is designed for complete 360-degree viewing of the fire.

Radiant Grate

This grate is designed with a front uplift of the logs in order to allow the radiation of the embers fallen on the hearth full heating exposure and potential. By placing the larger logs at the back of the grate, banking the ashes against the back of the firewall, and raking the coals forward, the resulting heat rays are not interfered with by the standard flatbed iron grate. This grate stands 12 inches high, 17 inches wide, and 17 inches deep and sells for $41. Small hearth ovens, rotisseries, grilles, and other items are also available.

Superior

Model 036 is a complete metal fireplace and chimney system available in 42 inches, 36 inches,

and 28 inches front opening. The firebox sides and throat are made of 20-gauge aluminized steel, the base of 18-gauge steel, the jacket 24-gauge steel. The chimney flue is a circular triple-wall flue with 10-inch, stainless-steel inner liner; outside diameter is 15 inches. The flue can be angled to a 30 degree offset from location of fireplace to chimney outlet. After the unit is installed, facing of used brick, flagstone, or rough rock is available.

Superior also makes ready-to-install electric fireplaces and metal free-standing fireplaces.

Thermograte

Like the others, this hollow-tube grate operates by natural convection. Cold air enters the bottom

tubes, is heated by the fire on the grate, thins and expands, and returns to the room through the top tubes. In such a system, the air can be heated to 600 degrees. Company tests indicate with Model 27-8 that a fire produces approximately 25,000 BTUs per hour of combined radiant heat and hot air delivered into the room. By adding the optional blower to the grate, up to 40,000 BTUs are said to be delivered per hour to the living area. The grate is made from .083-inch thick steel tubing, which, because cool air continually passes through them, can be heated 24 hours every day for 2 years without oxidation failure. The grates come with as few as 5 tubes, as many as 12, and up to 2 inches in diameter. The least expensive is $66; the most, $190. Optional ex-

tension tubes 6 inches and 12 inches long are available for extra-deep fireplaces.

Washington Stove Works

The Zodiac model free-standing fireplace is made with cast-iron top, bottom, and base, and

sheet-metal sides. The doors of the firebox and the ash pit are stainless steel and slide open and close in grooves. The fireplace comes in either 8-inch- or 10-inch-diameter flues. Excluding the flue, this model stands 38 inches high, is 28 inches wide, and has a shipping weight of 250 pounds.

The Drummer model fireplace is designed to resemble an oil barrel but is only about half the size. Its dimensions are 23 inches in diameter, 22 inches long, 33 inches high, and it weighs 120 pounds. It comes in black only and includes a grate, insulating back shield, and an ash pan.

Woodmack

The Heat-a-Grate is a hollow-tube air heater system with blower attached for forcing the warmed air from the pipes. The blower operates on 22 watts and mounts on either the left or right side of the grate. Models have from 5 to 10 tubes and weigh from 25 to 62 pounds. The largest size measures 26 inches high, 19 inches deep, and 26 inches wide, and costs $90. It operates by drawing in cool air from floor level, heating it from the wood burning on the grate, and sending the warm air out the top tubes into the room. The grate is guaranteed for 2 years.

DO-IT-YOURSELF STOVES

James Blackmore, who developed the barrel-shaped Yankee Woodstoves, first marketed do-it-yourself stove kits. They were simple designs with

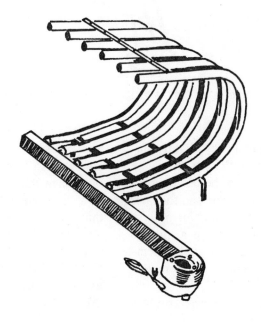

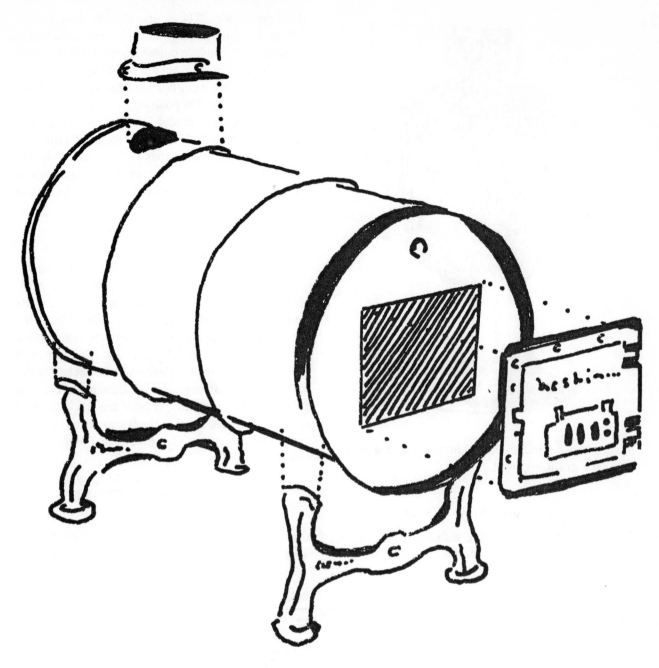

simple instructions and required only slightly unusual tools to assemble. He sold hardly any. Few people wanted to make their own, he discovered, because of the time involved for some and the lack of knowledge about using certain tools for others. So he took his own kits, put them on a miniassembly line in his small workshop, and assembled them himself. Then he sold them as ready-to-go stoves.

Do-it-yourself stoves do take some trouble, and unless you're handy with a cutting torch, or simply wish to have the adventure of making your own, then think twice before pursuing the project. It sounds great and romantic, but if you're all thumbs, you may end up freezing them come December before you can light up your masterpiece.

The basic homemade, dirt-cheap stove is usually made from old 30-gallon or 50-gallon oil drums that have been cleaned. These are usually called Yukon stoves after the old sourdough pioneers of Alaska who flocked to the gold fields at the turn of the century and made do with whatever was lying around.

Most of the Yukon stoves were oil drums laid on their sides and braced with stones so they wouldn't roll. One end was completely removed, and that was it. The fire heated the metal and added far more heat to the room than simply a dirt-bottom hearth.

Modification of this ultrasimple stove was to cut the side of a drum and attach a flat metal plate. This was the heating stove turned into a cooking stove as well, now flat enough to hold pots and frying pans.

Today Washington Stove Works has Yukon stove tops available for this and other purposes. The iron tops come in five sizes ranging up to 20 inches by 30 inches and weighing 40 pounds. These tops have a built-in flue hole and rivet holes already punched in.

Mounting one drum on top of another is possible. This allows wood gases from the bottom fire-bearing drum to escape into the upper chamber for additional burning. A side benefit is that more hot metal is exposed to the living area and more heat can thereby be generated.

A drum can also be used upright without any need for legs if good firebrick is placed under it. Cast-iron doors are marketed that can be welded to the bottom of the barrel with the flue attached to the back and the top.

In using the barrel in the standard Yukon stove design of laying the drum on its side, Washington Stove Works also manufactures oil drum conversion door and leg parts. The iron legs weigh 14 pounds and can be welded to the barrel to keep the stove away from combustible flooring. The cast-iron door measures 15 inches by 15 inches and the pipe collars come in 6-, 7-, or 8-inch sizes.

Whenever oil drum stoves are used, firebrick should be placed on the bottom and along the sides of the fire area. Instead of brick on the bottom, sand can be spread. These will help prevent oxidation of the metal and increase the number of years the stove will be safe and usable.

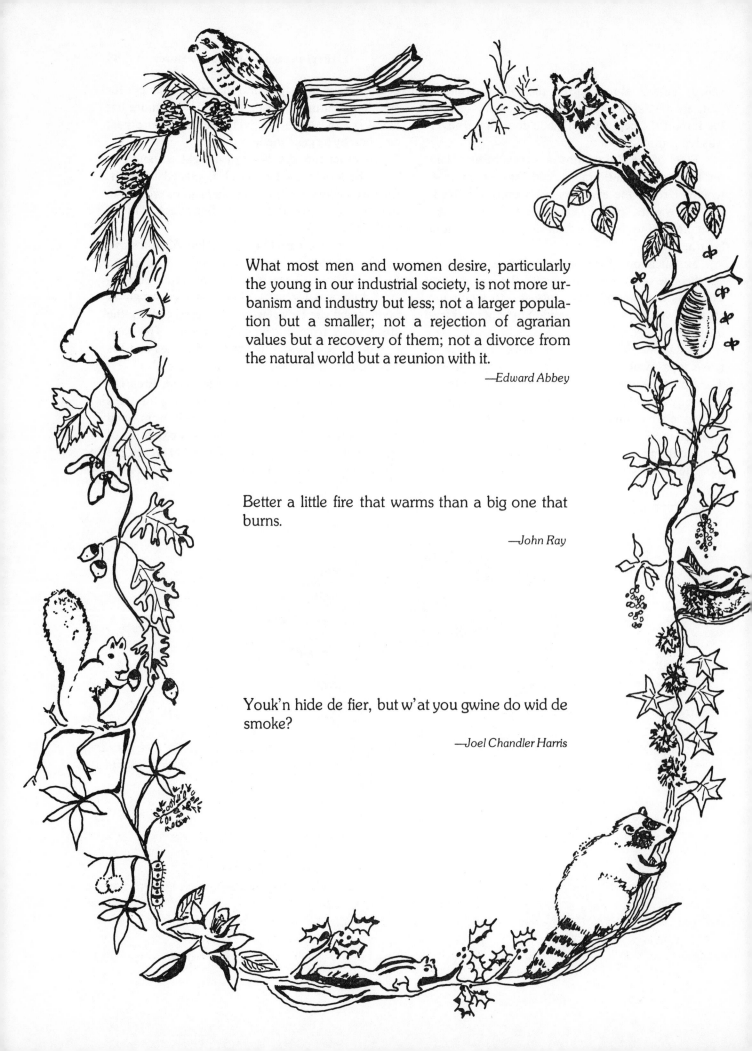

What most men and women desire, particularly the young in our industrial society, is not more urbanism and industry but less; not a larger population but a smaller; not a rejection of agrarian values but a recovery of them; not a divorce from the natural world but a reunion with it.

—Edward Abbey

Better a little fire that warms than a big one that burns.

—John Ray

Youk'n hide de fier, but w'at you gwine do wid de smoke?

—Joel Chandler Harris

Chapter 8

FIRE-BUILDING

If there's one great triumph in heating with stoves and fireplaces, it's building one-match fires. Somehow watching a calm, cool, experienced fire builder prepare a fire, strike one single solitary match, and set the blaze crackling and roaring toward flames and coals that last the entire night is a pleasure, a sign of someone who knows and has mastered the oldest heating source in history. Even more impressive is the person who, in late fall or early winter, prepares the first kindling of the season, lights up the stove with a single match, and keeps the home fires burning from November to March on that one lone magical fire stick. That's something.

Surprise! Anyone can build a one-match fire. Anybody can learn, but not everybody takes the time. No unauthorized secrets are involved and no deep, complicated, computer-printout equations are necessary. It's all a straightforward matter that takes an ounce of care to prevent a pound of trou-bles. A few rules, a few seconds of patience, and the art of one-match fires is yours forever.

But first—

HOW NOT TO BUILD A FIRE

You can build a fire with one match but not with one log, not for long, anyway. After the kindling is burned up, one log doesn't have enough hot feedback from itself to keep burning.

On the other hand, stuffing your stove with big six-inch thick logs and a piece of paper won't do any good either. Paper kindling will quickly curl up to ashes before enough heat is generated to raise the temperature to ignite the logs.

Even if the kindling and logs are balanced right, jamming it all together will not keep the fire going for long. It'll die out for lack of circulating air to keep the oxidation process in motion.

This ties in with the damper. No fire, or fire

time you couldn't figure out the square knot in Scouting days, then a few general hints are in order.

ASHES

As a rule, clear some, not all, the ashes from the firebox. Ashes are the mineral residue of wood that did not, and will not, burn. In some fireplaces the accumulation of ashes that have fallen through the grate can end up choking off the oxygen supply

builder, for that matter, will last long with the damper closed. If the wood gases and smoke have no escape hatch, they will back up from the flue and pour out the stove door and into the room.

Some fire builders can use half a box of kitchen matches and wonder why the kindling doesn't ignite. No wet kindling in the world will ever ignite, even if it's only slightly damp. It's futile to fight damp kindling. Search for something else and be happy.

One of the most dangerous ways in the world to build a fire is using kerosene or gasoline as a starter. People who use these are not only throwing caution to the wind; they're throwing their houses, and possibly themselves, into a hurricane of disaster. These highly flammable liquids are basically uncontrollable on a stack of wood. Stay away from them and stay alive.

So if your fire-building results in smoky backfires into your living room, if your kindling doesn't light and your logs glow red and then blink out like stoplights, if you find yourself on hand and knees, blowing yourself dizzy over the last vestiges of dying embers snubbing your desperate pleas and curses, making you feel the biggest failure since the

necessary for the fire to thrive. Without sufficient space beneath the grate for air circulation, the heart of the fire where the oxidation process is taking place, that is, on the immediate periphery of the wood itself, doesn't get enough fresh oxygen. As a result, the fire eventually dies or, at the minimum, struggles on like a broken-down Model A. Either way is frustrating. By removing some ashes air can reach the burning wood and continue to do so.

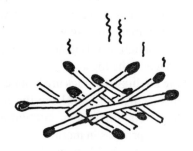

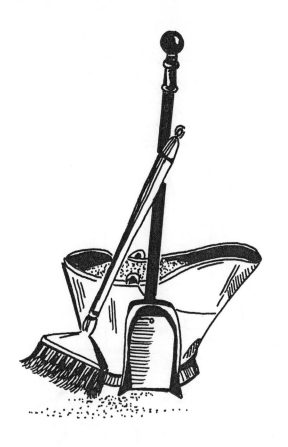

The same generally applies to stoves. By clearing out the ashes you also clear away unburnable obstacles to free-flowing flames. Even if your stove or furnace has an ash pit, empty it before it fills to the limit. Keep the interior free and easy for oxygen to find its way where it's not only welcome but absolutely essential.

Ashes are unburnable, but they do have advantages. One is that at proper height they can act in a way as reflectors to tighten overwide spaces between the fire on a grate and the bottom of a stove or fireplace.

More important, however, is using ashes as insulators. Before you stack your wood in preparing for a fire, decide if you want to save your coals later to last through the night. If you do and don't think you'll have enough ashes with only what will burn during the day and evening—which probably won't be enough—push a supply of old ashes to the side or rear of the firebox. When you retire for the night, maneuver your last bed of coals into the ashes and bank them against the back of the firebox. The ashes will insulate the coals from the air that would burn them faster than they would naturally die out.

STACKING

A roaring blaze begins with a tiny flame on a tiny splinter of wood. Take the hint. It's a little like the steps of a staircase—the lowest builds to the highest, the smallest to the largest. In other words, the quickest, surest fire results from pyramiding sizes one on the other.

Think ahead on this. Gather all sizes of your fuel together and have it on hand beside the stove or fireplace. That means that newspaper, the shavings, the splinters, the sticks, the logs. Lighting the newspaper and splinters and then having to run downstairs or outside for the logs is a waste of time and energy as well as probably putting the fire out.

One way of starting a fire is to add each of the fuel sizes separately as the fire catches and intensifies. This constant feeding of the fire works well enough, but it isn't as controllable and clean-feeling and doesn't give you a sense of building a sure-fire accomplishment.

The better way is to lay your fuel out on the grate all at once. First, the newspaper, then the kindling, the sticks, the small logs. As you do so, keep in mind that fire needs oxygen at all times. Instead of compressing the starter fuel into a tight mound, keep it loose; keep it full of small air tunnels and passageways.

One way is to stack the sticks and small logs in a log-cabin square pattern, alternating one on top of the other so that air spaces are also stacked together. When the fire catches, the flames then have access to air holes to feed themselves. Stacking the sticks in a teepee shape accomplishes the same effect.

Whatever the style, the simple but important point is to build the stack with plenty of room for

the first flames to move around. Nothing can kill a one-match fire faster than a solid block of wood, even if it's in pieces. You can't light a stove fire from a chunk of wood and one match anymore than you can light a tree trunk with one match.

By stacking your kindling and sticks in a loose but balanced pattern, such as a square, you also have an easier time placing the larger logs on when the fire develops its heat. The squarish structure will slowly collapse in the same general shape every time and you'll then have a predictable pattern to work with.

NEWSPAPERS

Some fire-building purists consider the use of newspaper a cheat in the art of starting a fire. Use only wood, they say. Besides, newspaper makes it too easy.

In the first place, newspaper is wood. In the second place, the art of building one-match fires becomes an art when the starting is easy. That's the whole point. Because something is easy doesn't mean it's wrong. On the contrary, experienced hands in any endeavor always choose the easiest way first because it's usually the fastest way to get where they want to go. Don't waste energy on method when the end result is more important.

So use newspaper as the base of your fire-building. It's handy and effective. Loosely crumple up about six to ten *half* sheets, depending on the size of the stove or fireplace, and lay them on the grate or base of the firebox. Make enough to be sure that your one match is itself Group the paper balls, but don't squash breathing air out of them. Arrange them and then flatten them slightly for the kindling.

KINDLING

Kindling is anything that kindles up a fire, that is, anything that burns readily enough to lead toward a hotter fire that will accept sticks and logs. This is the application of the Pyramid Principle: more of smaller pieces of wood burn fewer of larger pieces of wood.

In other words, the thinnest piece of wood, a

piece of newspaper, catches fire easily in order to burn a slightly thicker piece of wood, namely, shavings or twigs. These build up heat intensity enough to burn slightly larger pieces, such as sticks, which in turn build up enough heat to ignite the thicker logs.

This process can be used sequentially by feeding the newspaper fire with shavings and onward through the list to the logs, or it can be done all at once in a single pile—the better and easier way.

Kindling can include any dry, readily combustible material—field-mice nests, hair, broom hay, unraveled twine, sewing thread, any tinder that catches fire quickly for the next step. Usually, when you chop pieces of normally dry construction lumber into sticks for kindling, shavings and chips litter the basement floor. Gather up these chips and scatter them on the newspaper. They make excellent second- and third-stage kindling.

Another standby is to take dry sticks and with a field knife, or that dangerous tool the hatchet, slice at a slight angle partially into the stick at two- and three-inch intervals. Bend these wood slices outward but not off the stick. Do so on all sides of the stick. This way the growing fire can easily burn the

ragged edges on the sticks and gradually burn into the remaining main portion of the wood. Several of these fuzz-fire sticks assure a good running start on any fire.

Whatever kindling you use, the key is to keep the pieces touching each other but loose. Keep the oxygen valves open.

At this point, three small two- and three-inch-diameter logs can be loosely triangled on the kindling, or they can be added later when you feel secure that the fire is well on its way. Just be sure these small logs don't squash your kindling too heavily or chances are that the fire won't get past the newspaper-burning stage.

DAMPER

So far you haven't yet touched a match to kindling. That's the way it should be: everything should be set up completely before you strike the magic flame. That means having ready beside the stove or fireplace the wood you plan to put on the fire, once it gets crackling.

That also means making sure the damper to the chimney flue is open all the way. At all times when the firebox is not in use, the damper should be closed to prevent cold air, falling by natural convection, from pouring down the chimney through the open throat of the flue and into the house. A great deal of house heat is lost this way. Simply closing the damper prevents the loss.

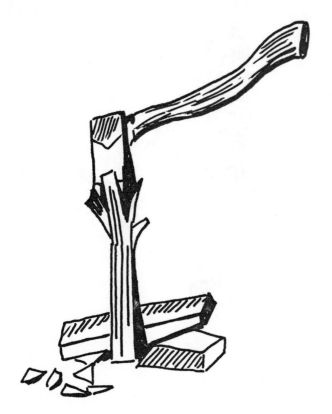

Make it a habit to open the damper before you strike the match. Wood gases and smoke must rise somewhere from the very beginning of the fire. An open damper creates a draft escape from the house. A closed damper creates a smoke rush into your face. All things considered, it's better not to pollute the fire builder.

PREHEAT THE FLUE

Since heat agitates, thins, and dissipates air upward, preheating the flue can create a faster first draft. One way to do this is to crumple very loosely a full-size newspaper page, hold it in one hand at one end toward the flue, if your stove or fireplace design allows you, light it, and let the heat rise and clear the flue of cold air. When the paper is nearly burned, drop it on the kindling and let that be your match for the fire bed.

This method, especially dropping it on the kindling, is not as controllable as a second way. If you're building your kindling pile and place logs on top, very loosely crumple one full-size newspaper page in a tent shape over the logs. Light it and let the heat do its work on the flue before the kindling catches hold. Sometimes the newspaper page burns out before it can reach the kindling beneath the logs, which turns the entire episode into a two-match fire. Other times the flames work well in both directions—up the flue for preheating, back down to the kindling to get the wood ignited.

Preheating the flue is a workable trick of the trade, although it is not overwhelmingly necessary. Many roaring one-match blazes, minus any smoke pouring into the room, work perfectly well without preheating the flue. Don't think you need it for all successful fires. It may be useful for some badly constructed, slow-drawing chimneys, which preheating can cure for starting fires, but otherwise consider this step one of the optional curiosities.

THREE-LOG FIRES

One-log fires don't last for long, two-log fires creep along before dying out too soon, but three-log fires can continue on indefinitely into the night.

Three-log fires, especially in fireplaces, should be your minimum structure. Three logs feed on each other far better than one or two alone, particularly if they are placed in a triangle with overlapping ends, close enough to concentrate intense heat in

the center of the triangle. Once enough heat is developed and three medium-size logs are red-hot halfway through their diameters, it's time to place one extra-large log directly on top of the triangle or, if in the case of a small stove, on top of the three coal-red parallel logs.

From then on it's home free. The last remaining parts of the three coal-hot logs will ignite the single large log and keep it flaming. If it dies down slightly, all it'll need is a stroke of the fire iron and maybe a quarter turn on its axis to expose fresh wood to the heat.

As the fire on the large log dies a little, simply replace one or two of the smaller triangle logs and watch the fire spurt ahead again.

MIXING GREEN AND DRY WOOD

The theory of using dry wood or high-resin-content wood to start a fire and to keep it long-lasting with dry heavy hardwood is true. But at a price. Wet wood produces creosote that clogs your flue and, if not removed, creates possible chimney fires. Wet wood also spits and pops because the high sap and moisture content trapped inside the wood cells is heated, expands, and finally bursts through the cells in miniexplosions. These loud bursts are what send parts of the burning logs shooting through the air. If no fire screen is in place, these sparks can land on your rug or floor and scar and burn them.

No individual fire can follow exactly a predictable time and flame table. Woods react differently not only according to their species but also from the size and cut, whether the bark is left on or not, whether the moisture content is 20 percent or 40 percent. It's impossible to pinpoint exactly how long three birch logs will last, but it is possible to anticipate general results.

Pine logs do burn hot and fast. Oak logs do burn slowly with low flames. All things being equal then, mixing a few small sticks of pine on your kindling can get your fire hot and intense enough for you to put on a hefty oak log much faster than if you had started your fire with small hickory logs. If this is what you want, then mixing pine and oak is workable.

However, mixing freshly cut logs of any species, either as a starter or follow-up with dry wood, is generally a mistake. The moisture content, high as it is at that point, must be boiled and vaporized away before the wood itself burns. That saps away potential fire energy from the real purpose of igniting the wood. It also fills your stove and fireplace with crackling and sparks, not necessarily bad but sometimes annoying.

Experience shows that it's better to mix green and dry wood, if they're going to be mixed at all, at the other end of the fire-making. Use dry 20 percent moisture-content wood to get the fire moving. Even once a good three-log fire is burning bright, put a large dry log on top. Then when that log is building up the hot coals and the fire is chugging along steadily, slip on a few medium-size, relatively green logs.

By mixing the green and dry wood at this point, the fire is intense enough to use the green wood to best advantage, namely, to prolong the fire without reducing its heat output too much. Many old-timers build their fires this way. It works for them and it can work for you. They found that, once the blaze is moving toward really hot coals, by adding some green wood (not necessarily freshly cut, just not air-dried the full way to 20 percent moisture content) they don't have to refuel the fire as often nor even stroke it back to life every fifteen minutes, as must be done with some wood.

No fire will get off the grate with all green hardwood. Normal kindling just does not burst into hot-enough heat to vaporize the moisture in the green wood and still have enough heat left over to keep the wood burning. All an all-green wood fire will do is flicker and sizzle and die out for lack of hot staying power.

This means that green wood, if used at all, must be used somehow in connection with dry wood. The only way to get to know how to mix them is to follow some of the above guidelines and experiment. No Chinese emperor will chop off your head if you fail, but you'll be a better fire builder and have a warmer house if you learn how to manipulate the two. It's worth the risk.

OXYGEN SUPPLY

Absolutely no fire burns well without sufficient oxygen to feed it. If the air intake valves in an airtight stove are locked shut, the fire will die. If a fireplace is loaded with ashes and the grate is half smothered in them, the fire will eventually die. It's even possible in an airtight house to have a fire stumbling along because it's eating up the oxygen supply available to it, let alone to the human creatures, faster than a fresh supply can be sucked toward it.

In such a tightly constructed house, open a window slightly to allow a flow of fresh air inside. It's good for the fire and it's good for you. In whatever type of wood stove, furnace, or fireplace, building and maintaining fires is easier if this simple but essential fact is ingrained in your methods: fire equals heat plus fuel plus oxygen.

convection. In airtight stoves, adjusting the air-intake valve can somewhat serve this purpose, but in fireplaces a bellows comes in handy. You can accomplish the same results with your lungs.

With open stoves and fireplaces, probably one of the most startling, unexpected methods of resurrecting a dying fire is the use of a single sheet of newspaper. This works if the stove or fireplace opening is the same or smaller than an opened full-size newspaper page.

Simply take the page and hold it flush to the top of the stove or fireplace opening. The rest of the page can freely hang down over the rest of the front. This blocks the air flow from the room directly into the fire. In turn, a strong draft is created by the already-heated chimney flue. The result is that the

REJUVENATING A FIRE

All fires fade away, no matter how perfect they are at the peak of their growth. All fires, however, can remain active indefinitely if fuel and oxygen are continually replenished. Unless you intend to have the fire die out, adding small sticks and logs to a larger-burning chunk of wood is one way to maintain the status quo.

Another is using a bellows to blow massive supplies of oxygen onto the coals, more fresh air than would ordinarily sweep into the fire by natural

chimney draft increases in the draw of air on the fire, which in turn circulates air through the fire and churns up the flames.

The first time you try this you will probably be surprised at how effective such a simple trick is. The newspaper page won't ordinarily catch fire, as it might appear, being so close to the flames. Instead, it'll send the flames upward toward the flue where the draft is pulling them as if they were on strings.

By slipping some dry kindling on the fire beforehand, this paper trick can rejuvenate a fire very quickly. It's also a good substitute for a bellows or blowing yourself silly, not to mention the startled oh's and ah's of those who haven't seen what a brilliant fire technician you are.

OVERNIGHT COALS

Some airtight stoves can hold a fire overnight without special treatment, but most stoves and fireplaces not designed for this require extra measures. The simplest and nearly foolproof method is burying hot coals in ashes.

To do so, plan to have a generous supply of coals ready. Burn enough hardwood toward the end of the evening to supply you the coals when you want them. If the logs aren't burned completely, simply knock some of the coals off just before you close up for the night.

You also must plan ahead to have a generous supply of ashes in which to bury the coals. Shovel half the ashes back toward the firebox. A corner is the best location, since it automatically provides two sides of the firebox for protection instead of one. Then shovel the hot coals together into the ashes, and after that bank the rest of the ashes over the coals.

Be sure the coals are well covered. This protects them from the air and from burning away too fast.

The coals should burn all night without any problem. If buried properly and out of touch of any logs or sticks, they have nothing to burn but themselves. They're perfectly safe.

In the morning simply rake out the coals, pile them together at the front of the firebox, lay sticks and small logs on them, and faster than instant coffee, you have a new stack of logs burning bright. Using coals this way is a good way to conserve your wood supply and still have one-match fires all season long. It's also a great way to take the chill off the early hours and a satisfying way to make friends with fire.

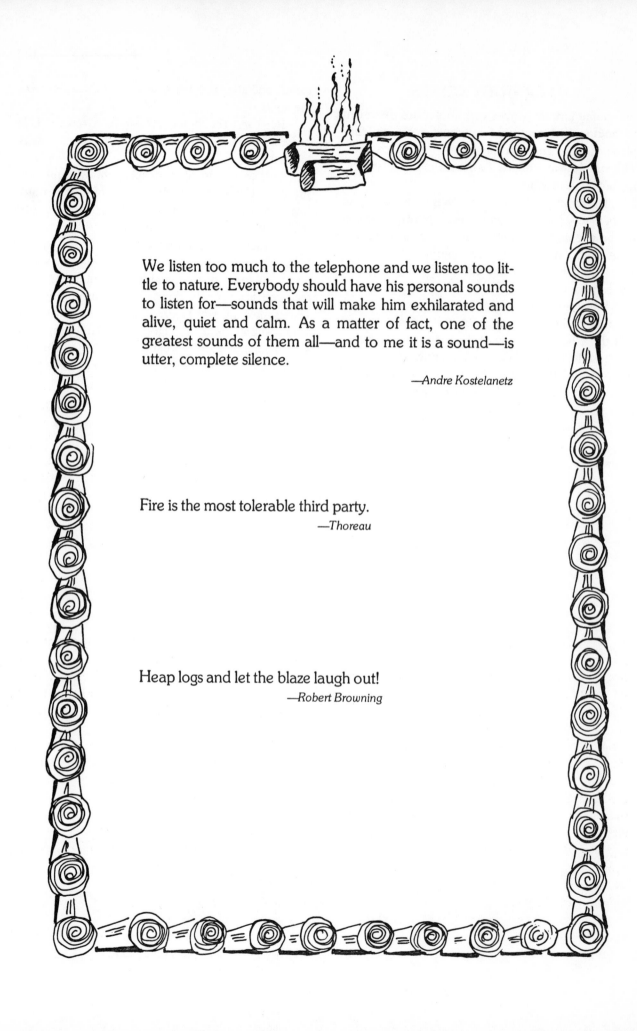

We listen too much to the telephone and we listen too little to nature. Everybody should have his personal sounds to listen for—sounds that will make him exhilarated and alive, quiet and calm. As a matter of fact, one of the greatest sounds of them all—and to me it is a sound—is utter, complete silence.

—*Andre Kostelanetz*

Fire is the most tolerable third party.

—*Thoreau*

Heap logs and let the blaze laugh out!

—*Robert Browning*

Chapter 9

GETTING THE MOST USABLE HEAT

Getting the most heat is not the same as getting the most usable heat. You can stuff your stove or fireplace with the hardest hardwood available and let the blaze roar out like the guns of Navarrone. That's getting the most heat. It's not any good to you, however, if the stove turns red hot or the fireplace boils into an inferno that's ready to burst the furniture into flame in the next three seconds.

Not only that, but making stoves and fireplaces a core feature of household life is its own pleasure. In the days before forced-air heating, the wood-burning cooking and heating stoves drew families together. It was around the warm kitchen stove that people gravitated, in rooms where the warm stoves were burning. The wood-burning stove in a sense became part of the family.

When central heating systems kicked the wood burners to the basements, a widespread sociological switch resulted. Members of the family could now go to their own rooms. They no longer gathered with each other as often nor did they have to take turns tending the fire, bringing in fuel wood, stoking up the flames. It was each man, woman, and child moving out of the warming circle that wood burners so subtly and neatly wove together.

Today people are finding that that special communal spirit is still possible and that, if the high price of fuel oil isn't an Arab blessing over the shoulder, then it certainly is a welcome crisis. Once again the wood-burning maker of family members together makes sense. Ah, progress!

Here are some ways to get the most potential from the old home fires burning.

PLACEMENT

Where your source of direct heating is located makes a difference. It's not always possible to place

your stove or fireplace exactly where you want, but if the choice is yours to make, make it carefully. The right location pays big dividends.

For example, if you can situate your stove in the center of the room, or at least away from a wall location, you have several advantages. Not only can the heat radiating from the stove strike out in a 360-degree circle, but family members and friends can sit or stand all around the stove. It happens time and again, especially at parties where guests inevitably congregate around the stove to talk and laugh and feel both the physical and spiritual warmth wood heat generates.

For a number of reasons, stoves cannot always be placed in the center of the room. If they must go next to a wall (and a minimum of 18 inches should be between the closest point of the stove and any combustible material), the next best spot is beside a masonry wall. Brick or stone take longer to heat up than wood or steel, but on the other end of the timetable they retain and radiate heat longer after the fire has died out. By placing a stove next to an

interior brick or concrete wall, the leftover heat that continues to pour forth is, in a way, bonus heat.

Because of this effect, corners of rooms can be bricked at the joining ends of two walls. Then the stove can be set at a diagonal angle to the corner and benefit from heating both bricked-in sides.

The metal free-standing fireplaces are relatively flexible as to where you can place them. If possible, stationing them outward from a wall is, like a stove, better. The effect of having the heat radiate in a wider circle results, but unlike the old-time house that ran the fireplace chimney up the center of the building, the metal flues, being fully insulated, do not retain and generate as much heat to other parts of the house.

A brick chimney in the center of the house, on

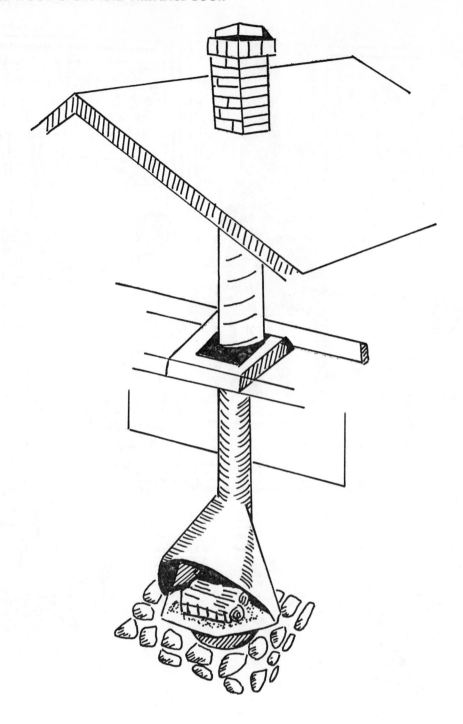

the other hand, benefits both the first and second stories. When a chimney is built on the outside of the house wall, as in most cases of recently constructed houses, heat that would otherwise enter the rooms is lost to the wind that chills the exposed chimney.

Since heat rises, one of the best places to situate a stove is in the basement. The heat gathers at the basement ceiling and seeps through to the general living area on the first floor.

If possible, another good location is fairly close to a stairwell. Again, since heat rises, stove heat finds its way by natural convection to the opening and climbs the stairs to the second story. Thinking in these terms can make full use of downstairs heat by having it useful after it has accumulated at the ceiling.

TIMING YOUR FIRE

One of the best ways to conserve your fuel-wood supply is burning it at the right time. It's not sensible to light up a fire when nobody's around to use it, but to judge the best time takes some experience and fire know-how.

In the first place, setting a fire beforehand (on dead coals) cuts down the time it takes between preparing the kindling and feeling the heat. Besides, having a fire bed set and ready to go hours or days before you light it, especially seeing the newspaper, kindling, and sticks in a fireplace, is a comforting sight. It gives you a good feeling of being well prepared and well planned. If you get in the habit of setting a fire early this way, if and when the previous one dies out, you're also setting up a consciousness of planning ahead—a key to using home fire efficiently and effectively.

Here's the magic principle: plan ahead by thinking backward. That is, if you want a plentiful hot-coal fire to peak in a fireplace at about 9 o'clock for friends to sit around after you've eaten dinner, then it's probably smart to start the fire burning well before you sit down to eat—maybe around 6 or 7 o'clock. Depending on the size of the fire, it takes

about two hours at the minimum to develop good oak coals. Some practice makes it easier to judge.

If you want your stove to be charged up hot for overnight heating, then figure what time you'll likely go to bed and plan accordingly—plan backward. Figure well ahead so that, in an airtight Scandinavian design, you'll have a bed of coals ready just before you retire. That way you'll have a fresh fuel supply just beginning and not have to lay new logs over half-burned ones.

Whatever, think in longer time spans. Get to know how long it takes for a fire to reach the peak you're working for. Start your fires in the same general structure and with the same general amount of fuel each time. In this way you can develop a reliable measurement on which to predict whether you want a flaming fire to peak at 9 o'clock or a shimmering, simmering bed of hot pepper-red coals.

FALSE DRAFTS

When a fire gets more air than is needed, it burns too fast and wastes your fuel. The oxygen supply is far less controllable in nonairtight stoves and fireplaces. Nevertheless, other than reconstructing the firebox or welding cracks together, replacing or adding asbestos rope around the door-jamb or carefully stuffing it in cracks can help reduce some excessive air intake.

False drafts on fires can also be located beyond the stove or fireplace. Too often cellars and basements are not checked for cold air pouring through open windows or cracks in old doors that have been forgotten from the summer. Some basements, being unlived in, are constructed without the care of the rest of the house. What sometimes results are misaligned door frames that seep cold air and windows that don't shut tightly. These small problems should be fixed.

Exhaust fans in kitchens and bathrooms should also be checked, to be certain they're closed. Winter air can easily get into the house through these vents if they're not sealed when not in use.

Attics should be checked. If windows or holes in the roof allow cold air to filter inside, and eventually to the ceiling and possibly through the attic staircase, then heat that could be warming you is being diverted to compensate for the maverick cold air that doesn't belong inside. Keep the mavericks outside.

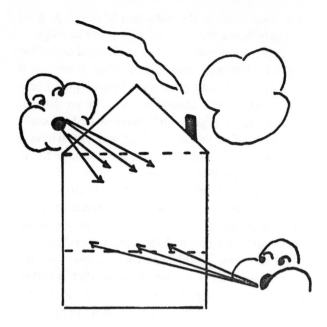

CLOSING OFF UNUSED ROOMS

The luxury of using wood-burning stoves and fireplaces to heat rooms that are not used is an expensive legacy from the cheap-oil space-heating era. It's unnecessary and it's absurd.

Instead of letting your hard-earned wood supply burn up for empty dens, closets, and storage rooms, it should be going entirely for where you live. At the very least, all it takes is keeping yourself aware of these spaces that can sap your stove and fireplace heat.

To close them off, simply close the doors. That'll block an amazing amount of heat from wandering around aimlessly. If the rooms are not used during the day but are at night, simply close the doors during the day and open them at night. Very simple. Very effective.

An added measure for rooms that are seldom, if ever, used is to further seal them off by stuffing old rags, towels, or blankets on the floor beneath the door. Also, if the door is out of sight and you don't mind the looks of it, hanging an old sheet or bedspread across the doorway does an extraordinarily good job of shielding the room. It may look flimsy, but it works.

FANS

Some house plans make the use of wood space heating more difficult than others. Either the natural circulation of air is obstructed by walls or too many general living areas are built into the design and therefore require too many stoves.

One way to get more mileage out of the same amount of heat is to use fans. This method is used very effectively by owners of Scandinavian stoves and American stoves that do not have optional blowers available.

All it takes is an inexpensive, quiet, low-powered fan bought in just about any department store. Set it near or above a stove, turn it to the lowest acceleration, and forget about it. It'll help push around the house the heated air emanating from the radiated furniture and walls.

Setting a fan near a doorway can also circulate warm air that otherwise gets clogged inside the room. Putting the fan as high as possible is best. That way the blades can whirl away at the heated air that has risen toward the ceiling.

Fans make ideal accessories that extend the usefulness of your heat. They can send warm air from one room to another and, if stove and stairwell

INSULATION

The longer you retain the heat from your stove or fireplace inside the house the better. To do that, your house should be an effective heat trap. A well-constructed house is the basis of getting the most usable heat from wood, and that means having a leakproof foundation, a leakproof roof, joints in the walls that are tight-fitting, and a host of other necessities that come with the actual building process.

You can, however, increase the insulating effect with some minor, easily done attention to details that do not require elaborate reconstruction. For one, make sure that your attic is protected from the cold sky falling through the roof by laying at least six inches of standard fiberglass insulation. This may cost some money outlay, but prorate the

are positioned right, even up and down the stairs from either the basement to the first floor or first floor to the second. If you find the right fans, they can be entirely unobstrusive and still do their job.

expense over the lifetime of the house in terms of reducing your heating bill either for fuel wood or oil.

In particularly cold climates, window shutters have long been abandoned—one of the all-time mistakes in home-heating controls. At one time window shutters were standard features on homes. Now, if they exist at all, they are functionless decorations that are merely exterior window-framing techniques. They usually have no hinges and can't be shut over the windows. They're useless.

Adding shutters on either the inside or outside of all windows, but especially on the windward side, can prolong heat retention immeasurably, particularly if they overlap the window so that no air can stream in around the edges. If you don't have shutters already on your house, seriously consider adding them. They are one of the legacies of yesteryear that should not have been forgotten.

Glass is a poor insulator and allows the cold to rush inside. If shutters aren't installed, at least think in terms of boycotting the cold as much as possible from marching through the windows. Simply pulling the curtains or shades at night, or in rooms that aren't used during the day, blocks the cold from entering and retards the heat from escaping. Air is one of the most effective insulators, so setting up an air trap between the glass and the curtain or shade, no matter how makeshift, does work.

Weather-stripping the doorjambs and windows is also important. However tight the walls of a house may be, the doors and windows of necessity must leak some air where they join the walls. Attaching metal stripping to the bottom of the door so that it touches the floor and lining the interior edges of windows with long thin rolls of claylike stripping are extremely effective.

Installing storm windows is essential in freezing climates. These double-pane windows use air as an insulator and keep out the cold so you can keep in the heat.

HOT WATER

Wood-burning stoves are ideal for reducing the amount of water taken from the hot-water tank powered by oil or electricity. A kettle of water can be kept on top of the stove at all times. It can be used as a humidifier as well as quick hot water for tea or coffee.

Water on the stove can also heat up enough to wash dishes, mop the floor, wash windows, clean the refrigerator. It's usually just the right temperature for washing behind your ears, besides. Every time you use hot water heated by your wood you save the cost of heating water, and pumping it through your faucet, by oil or electricity.

Systems such as Hydroearth can be installed to heat water in your fireplace. A grate with a cold-water inlet at the bottom heats the water as it circulates through the pipes that hold the burning logs. The discharge pipe then takes the hot water to the storage tank.

CLOTHES DRIER

With a wood furnace in the basement, taking advantage of the heat for drying your clothes is ideal. String up a clothesline or set up a drying rack and you have a natural drier for wintertime. If your stove is upstairs and you're not overly concerned about the appearance, then string up your clothes right there in the living room. Why not? It works and it saves money.

FOOD DRIER

Wood heat is good for drying fruits and herbs. Spread fruit one item deep on trays and set them above the stove or very close to it. Vegetables can be dried the same way. Tie herbs on a string above the stove so that they hang down high in the heat. Try to keep the distance of the fruits, vegetables, and herbs so that the temperature hovers around 110 degrees. A small thermometer can tell you that.

Wood stoves are good too to grow a yogurt culture. Placing the jars and bottles of milk wrapped in a sweater next to a stove sets the yogurt far faster than merely setting them in the kitchen window. Try it. You'll like it.

REMODELING YOUR FIREPLACE

Since fireplaces are notorious thieves of wood heat, anything you can do to improve their usual 10 percent efficiency is worth the effort. One way is to take Count Rumford's theories seriously, even though most fireplace builders these days don't.

Next to requiring a maximum four-inch throat opening (you can control that with modern

dampers) and a smoke shelf (which is normally already built in), constructing an angled fire-back wall and shallow hearth is probably Rumford's most important feature. In most cases, it isn't necessary to tear the present fireplace apart to improve heat radiation into your room. Usually, all you need to do is add more bricks to the back wall in order to make the fireplace shallower. Each situation is different, but with careful planning adding maybe two or three layers of brick and, if it isn't already slanted, angling forward the upper half is usually enough.

DUCT EXTENSIONS

Flue pipes are heated as the stove wood burns and releases the gases and smoke. It follows, then, that the longer the flue pipe, the longer the heat stays inside the house.

In the old days stovepipes were sometimes extended back and forth across the ceiling or up and down the wall before being hooked to the outside chimney. On most wood-burning stoves today it's possible to do the same.

Don't go wild on this, however. Too long an extension of the smokepipes can backlash on you. If the fire in the stove doesn't burn at its most efficient level, creosote builds up. Then if the flue pipe is extraordinarily long, the unburned wood residue is left in the flue inside the house. It coagulates into creosote and can seep back down the pipe, possibly clogging the smoke hatch or leaking through the flue joints. Either way, a higher risk of chimney fire results.

Nevertheless, thinking in terms of keeping the most safe heat inside the house as long as possible is part of the overall strategy of getting the most usable heat from your fuelwood.

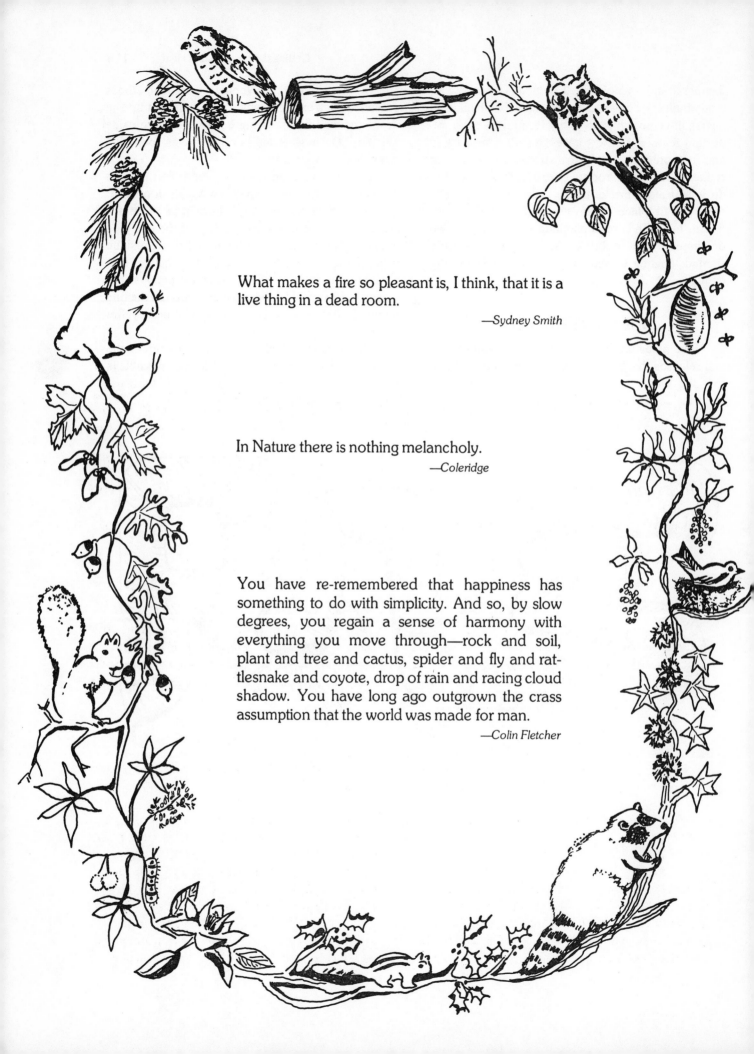

What makes a fire so pleasant is, I think, that it is a live thing in a dead room.

—*Sydney Smith*

In Nature there is nothing melancholy.

—*Coleridge*

You have re-remembered that happiness has something to do with simplicity. And so, by slow degrees, you regain a sense of harmony with everything you move through—rock and soil, plant and tree and cactus, spider and fly and rattlesnake and coyote, drop of rain and racing cloud shadow. You have long ago outgrown the crass assumption that the world was made for man.

—*Colin Fletcher*

Chapter 10

STOVE AND FIREPLACE MAINTENANCE

Any garden, machine, farm, or household that is cared for is going to be easier to work and enjoy. Each of them is going to produce more, look better, provide better products, and give you a sense of pride. An added bonus is that keeping them in top shape makes them run smoothly at the time you want to use them. Also, continuous, good maintenance assures the long life of your land, car, or house in addition to keeping the cost of operation down. So it pays to hoe out the weeds, lube your four-wheeler, feed the soil, or repair leaky roofs.

It's the same for stoves and fireplaces. Good maintenance on a regular schedule is well worth the small effort. Fortunately, heating your house with wood doesn't involve highly complicated mechanical components that demand constant attention. Stoves and fireplaces are relatively straightforward, simple tools that require only a little time now and then to keep tuned to perfection. Their tolerances for something to go wrong are wide enough that a tight timetable of maintenance isn't necessary at all. What is necessary, if you want top burning efficiency and safe operation, are periodic checks to see that the next time you strike up a match means pleasure, not problems.

ACCESSORIES

Other than makeshift implements, some basic tools are handy to have around when it comes time to stoke up the fire or clean the firebox.

The essential tool is a poker of some kind, one made of a single length of iron and hooked at the end to push and pull logs into place. With a poker you can rearrange the fire easily and stir up the coals. It's also used for opening and closing dampers when the handle is placed close to the fire and becomes too hot to touch with your fingers.

Other handy tools include a pair of tongs, big iron tweezers, for dealing with burning logs that re-

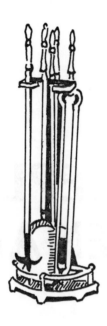

quire better leverage than a poker can provide. A small fine-brush broom is good for sweeping away the ashes—a lot better than a whisk broom or fanning them with a magazine. An ash scoop or small shovel is ideal for removing ashes from a fireplace or Franklin stove, even a Scandinavian stove, although a solid-end rake is more feasible for the imports.

A bellows is not necessary, especially if you're a one-match fire builder of experience. But if you like the shape and spirit of them, they do add a nostalgic sight to your living room.

A fire screen for Franklin stoves, masonry fireplaces, and free-standing fireplaces is really not an accessory. It's a necessity and should be used. It can save your rug, and maybe your house, from flying sparks.

A woodbox is handy and can be either any old box or coal scuttle you picked up from the town dump, or a handmade shellacked piece of proper furniture. If all else fails, lay a fully opened section of the Sunday newspaper on the floor and stack the logs on this.

Any of the other equipment and products on the market are usually more gimmicks than tools and not really needed. You're better off to keep the fire-building area clean and simple.

BLACKING

Over a period of time, black iron stoves fade, become rust-marked or discolored. Enameled porcelain stoves, on the other hand, don't react this way even to constant use and therefore don't need brightening up.

To brighten up your black iron stove with a good finish, compounds in both liquid and solid form are sold at good wood-stove shops and hardware stores. The Portland Stove Foundry of Maine distributes a 3.5 ounce tube for about $1.30 that is designed exclusively for black iron stoves. Other examples of blacking include Blue Ribbon liquid polish at about $2.00 for a pint and Presto Stove Polish, a wax, for about 90¢ for 6 ounces.

These and others are used basically the same way. The one important direction for all of them is that the wax or polish must be applied to a cold stove. A soft cloth such as an old flannel shirt is good to use to apply the compound. Then with a clean dry cloth, luster up the stove to the bright, shiny black beauty it was when it first came from the factory.

ASHES

Take no chances with ashes. Always—but always—shovel them into a metal container, never a paper bag or cardboard box. Ashes make good insulators of coals for a surprising length of time. If you happen to shovel some ashes and live coals together into a paper bag, you could also be shovel-

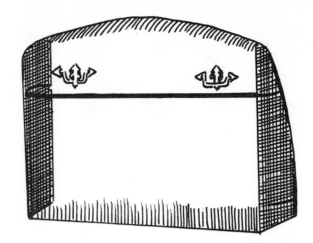

ing in the possibility that the coals could ignite the bag, which could ignite nearby newspaper or wood or furniture, which could ignite the entire house. Eliminate that possibility altogether by always transferring ashes into metal buckets or cans.

Keep in mind that ashes are composed of up to 70 percent lime, along with relatively minor traces of potash and phosphorous. Because of this, they make excellent flower and vegetable garden fertilizer if you need to balance an acid soil, and usually you do if you live east of the Mississippi River. Spread the ashes over the plot (or your lawn) and rake or water them in just as you would with a bag of commercial lime.

In its purest form lime is calcium oxide. Mixed with water it forms calcium hydroxide to produce slake lime, the familiar white powder. This is the material used in whitewash and mortar and to balance an overacid soil. It does pay to save the winter wood ashes in, for example, a metal garbage can for enriching your planting soil the following spring. Besides, recycling your stove and fireplace residue keeps the organic process of burning wood for heat complete from tree to match to ashes.

CREOSOTE

The accumulation of creosote on the sides of the chimney flue results from slow-burning fire—one reason why good, dry hardwood is preferable to green softwood. Such wood keeps the fire hot and burning as many of the wood by-products as possible before they go up the chimney. Slow-burning low-combustion fires in either stoves or fireplaces yield more pyroligneous and acetic acids that mix with whatever wood moisture is not fully evaporated by a relatively cool fire. This mixture is creosote.

Since the fire is comparatively cool, the flue is cool as well. As a result, the creosote condenses, clings to the flue walls, and hardens. In its liquid state, it can seep through the chimney lining if cracks are present and pose even greater fire danger to the house. (A high leaping-lizard tongue blaze is just as bad as a slow-burning one, since the flames shooting up the flue can set the creosote on fire.) Creosote is extremely volatile. If it catches fire, it burns rapidly and hotly. It is a real danger that must be reckoned with.

Fortunately, creosote is easily prevented, al-

though not so easily removed. First, learn to control the intensity of the fire, that is, by not letting it burn too slowly as well as not letting it blaze forth like a volcano. Secondly, clean the chimney.

CLEANING THE FLUE

Most chimneys need only infrequent attention, especially if they are well built and relatively new. Extra attention should be paid to the older houses that show signs of brick mortar falling out where smoke can escape either into the house or outside.

Checking the chimney once a year before or after the long winter burning season usually is sufficient for a wide range of situations.

The black-faced chimney sweeps from the Mary Poppins era are gone. In their place come the professional cleaners who vacuum the chimney clean like a rug. No fuss to worry about; no soot to see. However, unless your wood fuel is extremely green and ill-controlled, chances are that paying a commercial outfit is really unnecessary.

You can clean your own chimney without too much problem and only a little soot in your eye.

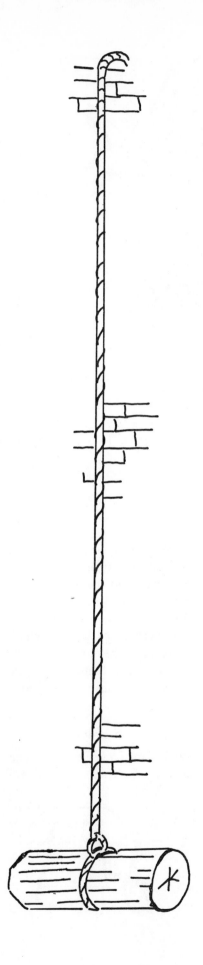

Your goal is to scrape as much of the tars and ashes and soot and general creosote from the sides of the flue. One way to pry loose the hardened material is to attach a blade of some kind to a pole, scrape off the creosote, let it fall to the ash pit, and later carry it off to the dump.

Another is to tie a long rope to a sturdy bush or small tree and with a friend who likes dark adventure pull it up and down the chimney. Having the bush or tree fit snugly against the flue walls gives it the pressure to remove some of the soot.

Tying a rope to a log is another effective way. From the chimney top, drop the log down and bang it against the walls the length of the flue. You can do the same with a log and chain on a rope.

While you're on the roof, check the screen on top of the flue escape. If it is clogged with soot and ashes, by all means clean it off. A dirty screen can reduce the draft and cause a backfire of smoke into the house.

If you don't already have a screen on the chimney top, then think about getting one. They not only prevent twigs and branches from falling down on a stormy night but also block birds from nesting inside. Bird nests create the same back-draft problems as a clogged screen. Birds themselves have been known to fly all the way down the chimney to the fireplace and out into the room, sooting up the house in the process. If you do need a screen, get a firm one that has large mesh openings to keep the draft free and easy.

CHEMICAL CLEANERS

Chemical chimney cleaners generally work satisfactorily in the part of the flue closest to the fire. Their effectiveness diminishes rapidly for much of the upper half of the chimney, if not becoming totally worthless. For this reason, don't rely entirely on them if you have creosote problems. They can, however, be used moderately in conjunction with other cleaning methods.

Chimney Sweep brand is a mixture of sodium chloride and copper sulfate. For stoves sprinkle half a cup on a red-hot fire with the drafts closed. Then open the drafts and repeat for four days, reducing the process later to once a week. For fireplaces half a cup is sprinkled on a red-hot fire that carries the chemical up the walls of the flue so it can eat at the creosote. Doing this twice a week is recommended

for a fireplace in continuous use. The risk is that the chemical cleaners can cause fire hazards since they're designed to burn away the soot.

CHIMNEY FIRES

If by chance you have a fire in your chimney—and the chances are remote—act quickly. What usually happens is that the creosote ignites with a burst. To feed its suddenly insatiable appetite for oxygen, air rushes with a roar up the chimney.

Your first move is to telephone the fire department. Such a fire often moves to other parts of the house. Take no chances. Get help at once and later have expert opinions that the fire is totally out in the chimney and other parts of the house, such as the roof, attic, rafters, outside walls.

Meanwhile, you can try to extinguish the fire by dumping large quantities of coarse salt on the fire in a stove or fireplace. Close all the drafts on a stove to block as much oxygen to the flue as possible. For a fireplace you can soak a blanket or large towel and cover the fireplace opening, again blocking as much of the draft intake of oxygen to the fire as possible.

Whatever you do, get out of the house if the fire happens to spread into the general structural part of the house. Fire is dangerous enough, but smoke and invisible carbon monoxide are what cause 80 percent of the 6,000 deaths in the 700,000 fires inside American homes each year. You can build or buy another house but not another you.

SAFETY

Although smoke detectors for homes are not as reliable as many fire chiefs would like, they do add

an extra measure of protection They should be placed as close to the bedrooms as possible, since most fires in the home that result in death occur between 10 P.M. and 6 A.M.

One model is the SmokeGard 800A Early Warning Smoke Detector. It is operated by six 1.5 volt AA alkaline batteries and therefore takes no electricity. The batteries can last up to 18 months,

but the mechanism is designed to alert you when the power is fading. When smoke hits the detector, an 85-decibel alarm sounds. This is the time a small fire extinguisher in the house is important to have readily accessible.

Horror stories are easy to find, such as the family of six that died from carbon monoxide by burning charcoal inside the house without the windows or doors cracked open. Or the seven young children who died by overfiring a stove and setting the walls on fire. Or the family whose house wall and rug were burned because their stove was too close to combustible material. Or the house that burned because the wood joists ignited when two overfired fireplaces overheated the chimney. Or the man who was burned when he squirted lighter fluid on hot coals.

These are actual cases that the National Fire Protection Association points out could happen again if certain minimum precautions aren't taken. For instance, keep at least 18 inches between a wood-burning stove or fireplace and any combustible material. That includes wood walls, stacks of newspapers, boxes of matches, pillows, rugs, chairs, brooms, anything at all remotely possible that can ignite. Stand a stove on asbestos flooring or brick. Fix an asbestos board on the wall behind the stove. Remember that our bodies malfunction at only 104 degrees and are destroyed at a few higher degrees, while pine wood ignites at 900 degrees. We aren't much competition for fire.

Never use inflammable liquids to start a fire, including barbecue lighter, cigarette lighter fuel, and especially kerosene and gasoline, both of which can be catastrophic next to fire. They can flash and unleash their fury against you and your house.

By merely remaining aware that fire can be a destroyer as well as a protector, the chances of doing anything foolish automatically are reduced. You end up feeling safe because you feel secure about using fire. Above all, you appreciate that dealing directly with fire can go either way for you—good or bad—but if you keep it in the stove and fireplace you can discover as you never have before that fire really is a gift of the gods.

ADDRESSES

Ashley Automatic Heater Co.
1604 17th Ave. S.W.
P.O. Box 730
Sheffield, Alabama 35660

Atlanta Stove Works
Atlanta, Georgia 30300

Better 'n Ben's
P.O. Box 766
Old Saybrook, Connecticut 06475

Birmingham Stove & Range Co.
P.O. Box 2647
Birmingham, Alabama 35202

Bow & Arrow Stove Co.
14 Arrow St.
Cambridge, Massachusetts 02138

Chimney Heat-Reclaimer Corp.
53 Railroad Ave.
Southington, Connecticut 06489

Eagle Industries Inc.
P.O. Box 67
Madison, Ohio 44057

Edison Stove Works
P.O. Box 493
Edison, New Jersey 08817

El Fuego Industries
Main St.
Oakville, Connecticut 06779

Fire-View
P.O. Box 370
Rogue River, Oregon 97537

Fisher Stoves
504 So. Main
Concord, New Hampshire 03301

Golden Gate Fireplaces, Inc.
2391 Spring St.
Redwood City, California 94063

Heat-catcher
Lassy Tools, Inc.
Plainville, Connecticut 06062

Heatilator Fireplace
Mt. Pleasant, Iowa 52641

Hydroearth
Box 382
Ridgeway, Pennsylvania 15853

Jotul
Kristia Associates
P.O. Box 1461
Portland, Maine 04101

King Products Division
P.O. Box 730
Sheffield, Alabama 35660

Lance International
Box 562
Bloomfield, Connecticut 06002

Locke Stove Co.
114 West 11th St.
Kansas City, Missouri 64105

Majestic Company
Huntington, Indiana 46750

Malm Fireplaces, Inc.
368 Yolanda Ave.
Santa Rosa, California 95404

National Fire Protection Association
470 Atlantic Ave.
Boston, Massachusetts 02210

Old Stove Co.
P.O. Box 7617
Dallas, Texas 75209

Portland Franklin Stove Foundry
57 Kennebec St.
Portland, Maine 04104

Radiant Grate
31 Morgan Park
Clinton, Connecticut 06413

Riteway Manufacturing Co.
P.O. Box 6
Harrisonburg, Virginia 22801

Shenandoah Manufacturing Co.
P.O. Box 839
Harrisonburg, Virginia 22801

SmokeGard
140 S. Union Blvd.
Lakewood, Colorado 80228

Styria
The Merry Music Box
10 McKown St.
Boothbay Harbor, Maine 04538

Superior Fireplace Co.
4325 Artesia Ave.
Fullerton, California 92633

Thermograte Enterprises, Inc.
51 Iona Lane
St. Paul, Minnesota 55117

U.S. Department of Agriculture
Forests Products Laboratory
P.O. Box 5130
Madison, Wisconsin 53705

United States Stove Co.
South Pittsburg, Tennessee 37380

Vermont Techniques, Inc.
P.O. Box 107
Northfield, Vermont 05663

Vermont Woodstove Co.
307 Elm St.
Bennington, Vermont 05201

Washington Stove Works
P.O. Box 687
Everett, Washington 98201

Woodmack Products, Inc.
850 Aldo Ave.
Santa Clara, California 95050

Yankee Woodstoves
Bennington, New Hampshire 03442

INDEX